Overcom
GENERATI
to Get the Most Out
of Your Workplace

MANAGING THE OLDER EMPLOYEE

Communicate

Motivate

Innovate

Casey Hawley, MA

Avon, Massachusetts

Published by Adams Business, an imprint of
Adams Media, a division of F+W Media, Inc.
57 Littlefield Street, Avon, MA 02322. U.S.A.
www.adamsmedia.com

ISBN 10: 1-59869-858-3
ISBN 13: 978-1-59869-858-9

Printed in the United States of America.

J I H G F E D C B A

Library of Congress Cataloging-in-Publication Data
is available from the publisher.

This publication is designed to provide accurate and authoritative information
with regard to the subject matter covered. It is sold with the understanding
that the publisher is not engaged in rendering legal, accounting, or other
professional advice. If legal advice or other expert assistance is required, the
services of a competent professional person should be sought.
—From a *Declaration of Principles* jointly adopted by a Committee of the
American Bar Association and a Committee of Publishers and Associations

Many of the designations used by manufacturers and sellers to distinguish
their product are claimed as trademarks. Where those designations appear in
this book and Adams Media was aware of a trademark claim, the designations
have been printed with initial capital letters.

This book is available at quantity discounts for bulk purchases.
For information, please call 1-800-289-0963.

Dedication

This book is dedicated to my father, Sam Fitts, who consistently advocated and mentored younger generations throughout his career and in his personal life. He could recognize potential and gifts, give practical encouragement and inspiration, and was not shy about contributing a good kick in the pants when needed.

My father was a highly decorated war hero, seeming to always be where the most mortally dangerous battles were happening throughout his military career. He was part of the landing at Normandy, with death creating a 360-degree panorama around him; he cunningly hid outnumbered troops in Italy. He was in a horrific plane crash, immediately got on another plane though injured, and promptly returned to battle with no recuperation time. He received several Silver Stars and numerous other special medals for his bravery, but he kept those accolades to himself for many years. His love for his family, especially my beautiful mother, Sue, led him to the decision not to bring the details of the intense action he saw in the wars into our lives. Instead, he told us an improbable tale of doing endless kitchen patrol for his entire time at war, saying that he never saw any action, and for over thirty years none of us questioned it.

A few years ago, my son Houston became an avid student of World War II history. He would question my father endlessly about the generals, the maneuvers, and the action. Soon it became apparent that my father had been on the front lines for some of the most decisive and costly battles of several wars. Perhaps enough time had elapsed, perhaps with my mother's Alzheimer's he no longer had to protect her from the horrors he had seen, but my father finally told us the true story of his wartime experiences.

All this to say that this extraordinary man did not return from what he had seen (and it was a lot) bitter or negative. He came back with an eye for seeing talent in the younger men and women who worked with him in sales. He was the most proactive mentor and advocate of young professionals I have ever seen, long before mentoring became a trend. Perhaps because he had daughters, he especially championed women, and made sure they were treated with respect in an era when women in the workplace were not always valued for what they could offer professionally. My dad made sure the value of these women was known and rewarded. He instilled a can-do attitude in his daughters, granddaughters, grandsons, and nieces because he, this great man, thought there was greatness in them.

I dedicate this book to him because he taught me to see greatness in others and to know that greatness can cross generational, racial, and every other kind of line.

Thank you, Dad.

Casey Fitts Hawley

Contents

Introduction

No one takes a job to fail. That principle was the first one I was taught as a young management consultant about to be turned loose in organizations across the United States, Canada, and Brazil. So if we all—young, old, and in-between—want the same success, efficiency, and performance, why is working together so challenging at times?

Generational differences account for part of the mystery of how we are all charging headlong toward the same business destination yet wind up on different paths along the way and distant from one another. I would like to stress that generational differences are just one part of a myriad of differences that keep the workplace from being deadly dull. We are different from our coworkers, not just because we are Generation Y and they are Boomers, but because we lived over a deli in an urban setting and they lived a fairly isolated life on a dairy farm in North Dakota. We look at things differently not just because of that twenty-year age gap but also because of the gap created because we were brought up in a nuclear family with six brothers and sisters and our coworker was an only child of a single mom. We differ from that person we manage because her thoughts are rich and creative, while we are lightning fast with concrete answers but not so much with conceptual ones. The list goes on.

Generational differences, just like racial, gender, and ethnic differences, make us interesting. Just like you found that girl in your fifth-grade class fascinating because her mother let her wear a lot of makeup (something your mother thought inappropriate) or how you found that guy in sixth grade with the punk bands stamped on his T-shirts really cool, so we find people of other generations interesting because they do things differently at times. You may not necessarily want to do or say or wear what they do, but they do lend variety to the landscape of your life.

The workplace is much more exotic than your high school and college were, and part of that texture and variegated landscape comes from the four generations present on any given day. For the first time in history, four generations (by some counts five) are represented in the workplace simultaneously. This is a huge boost to the flavor and vibrancy of our work lives. I see it almost like the first explorers who brought spices from China and India to the Europeans. The differences made day-to-day fare more exciting, added depth and zest to certain foods, and drew out the piquancy and sharpness that were at times surprising but ultimately enriching. Generational differences add the same piquancy, sometimes the same surprises, but certainly the overall enhancement to the work lives of Generation X and Y employees.

Not Your Parents' Workplace

For almost a decade, gurus, management consultants, and human resource analysts have been anxiously anticipating this day. Generation X and even Generation Y are now managing the Baby Boomers. Almost universally, experts and prognosticators predicted conflict and resentment. The news is in and it is good. Things are going well—very well—as more Generation X and Y managers lead organizations and manage older workers.

Still, your workplace is so radically different from the workplace described in many traditional management books that you need information that is new, current, and relevant to your unique situation. After all, this is the first time that four generations are working side-by-side, with the least senior employees often managing the most senior employees. This is not your parents' workplace, at least not the one they started with. Many of the issues you will be dealing with will be generational, and the following chapters offer a variety of solutions to help you tackle the management issues of today.

Chapter 1 offers an overview of the main issues that make the Baby Boomers different in some ways from their Generation X and Y managers. These broad brush strokes give only a general picture of how the older generation developed such a strong identity that affects their work style. Chapter 1 also offers some insights into the predominant work styles and traits of Generations X and Y in contrast to the Boomers as a backdrop for the chapters to come.

Three Tools for Solving Management Challenges

Managing the Older Employee offers three unique tools to give you insight into how to manage older workers to achieve amazing results and create a high-performing organization. First, the XYBoom Survey delivers some enlightening results from a survey of 557 Generation X and Y managers. These younger managers tell you what they have learned about being successful and, perhaps just as important, what they have learned from their failures. The results from the objective section of this survey are summarized in Chapter 2.

Next, Chapters 3 through 9 identify seven major gaps that exist between younger managers: timing, technology, communication, motivation, office politics/respect, diversity, and innovation. Each of these chapters begins with solid strategies to make you and your employees more successful, all derived from the experiences of the author, who has been a successful management consultant for over twenty years. The management strategies for bridging the gaps included are highly effective and easy to implement.

More exciting are the offerings that follow: the ideas, solutions, and advice for success from Generation X and Y managers just like you. This is advice delivered by your peers who face the same challenges you do every day. The XYBoom Survey asked respondents to write in their approaches to bridging the seven gaps. These very candid respondents offer a wealth of advice about what they have tried and what succeeded, as well as what didn't. Excerpts from the actual comments made by these Gen-XY respondents are included. At the end, all this leading-edge advice, the best ideas from the younger managers, as well as the author's strategies are summarized in a list of "Dos and Don'ts."

The book concludes by looking forward to what you need to know to be successful in the future workplace after the older workers retire. Boomers hold vital information in their heads that you must be sure you appropriate before they leave the work force. Boomers are unparalleled in areas such as negotiations, nonverbal communication, and critical thinking. These are skills that you can acquire if you work very intentionally with the Boomers while they report to you. These skills are particularly important as business goes global. You may have been able to be successful up until now without these abilities, but they are necessary in some countries, some industries, and even in some companies you may work for in the future.

Each chapter offers ideas and strategies for making you the manager you want to be. Integrating these approaches into your own unique style will make you more successful in your organization, valued by the people you are leading and developing, and well satisfied with your results in one of the most difficult roles of all, the role of manager.

This is not your father's management book. It was influenced and formed by Generation X and Y managers, and they are incredibly honest and generous with their advice. So experiment, adapt, and try on different approaches to transform the older workers in your life so that they are able to achieve the results you want. Meanwhile, you will be creating a workplace atmosphere that is collaborative and supportive

CHAPTER 1

Fundamental Truths— What Generation X and Y Managers Need to Know about Baby Boomers

Is there something about a Boomer employee that is driving you crazy? Are you feeling completely stymied in your efforts to motivate an older worker to support the changes you have recommended or to try a new approach to work? Believe it or not, there is a method to their maddening behavior. Boomers may not be completely right in their attitudes that may clash with yours at times, but older workers have their reasons for believing what they do about how the workplace should operate. After all, they know "The Rules," and they may feel you have not been around long enough to know them all. An older worker's balkiness about getting onboard with your latest initiative may be his way of trying to teach you something he feels you need to know. But what Boomer employees call "the Rules," you may call "old school."

Which Generation Are You?

GENERATION	BIRTH YEARS
Boomer	1947–1965
Generation X	1966–1977
Generation Y or Nexters	1978–1995

*According to U.S. Census 2000

Why Do Boomers Think Their Way Is the Right Way?

Some say the Boomers were the first generation to have greater opportunities to make choices. In previous generations, if your father had a farm you were usually destined to be a farmer. If your father was the town doctor, you were likely to take over his practice after your inevitable medical education. Can you imagine that? What if your career had been predestined by your father's (certainly not your mother's) choice of occupation?

In addition, some people from this groundbreaking generation who previously had almost no choice about their roles in the world were given fresh starts—notably women and African Americans. A huge paradigm shift occurred when moms were taken out of the kitchen during World War II and asked to work in factories to make munitions and supplies. These mothers of Boomers learned that women can indeed make contributions to the workplace and that this work can be satisfying and rewarding in many ways. Similarly, the war somewhat leveled the workplace playing field for all races, showcasing the leadership skills of many African Americans and providing funding for their education. The result was the influx of both women and African Americans into the workplace. The stage was set for a brave new workplace for the Boomers.

The older members of Generation Y, consisting of those individuals born between 1976 and 1995, are entering the workforce now. With 70 million members, Generation Y is almost as large a demographic group in the United States as the baby boomers, a group that boasts upwards of 76 million individuals.

—*Julie Wallace,*
"After X Comes Y—Echo Boom Generation Enters Workforce"

New choices and exciting opportunities made the Boomers very aware that they were the generation who would change things. While some were burning bras and flags, most Boomers were changing the workplace. You can understand, then, why it is difficult for Boomers when you lump them into the same category as earlier generations such as the Traditionalists or Veterans. Boomers are the agents who ushered in the most radical social and marketplace changes in American history. The Boomer whom you view as not open to change may have been the first coed at her university to have an African American roommate. Or the older manager you think cannot be innovative may have sponsored the first domestic abuse conference or child abuse awareness campaign your city has ever had, because topics like that were not discussed openly in a Boomer's childhood. The key to understanding *how* the Boomer is thinking is to look at *why* he thinks as he does. This chapter offers some fundamental truths about Boomers and contrasts their most prevalent traits to those of Generations X and Y. You may, however, find some sweeping generalizations that may not apply to your favorite Boomer employee. These generalizations are simply offered to give you a general context for the older generation.

Boomers are generally not clock-watchers and have a strong work ethic.

They are likely to arrive early for meetings, perhaps really early. If you want some good conversation time with a Boomer that will bolster his respect for you, get to a training class or meeting about 45 minutes early; try to get there prior to the Boomer's arrival. He will be completely knocked out. The conversation will flow more freely and he will be more open.

✓ *Management lesson learned:* If you are frustrated by the Boomer's lack of technology dexterity, ask yourself if his work ethic compensates for it. Coverage of schedules from early to late is important in many businesses. Does the older worker bring another kind of value by showing up early?

We all get tasks completed in different ways. If the Boomer is weaker than younger employees in some area of expertise, ask yourself if he also balances the team by his contributions in other ways such as offering coverage, continuity for customers, or a heritage of departmental knowledge that would be difficult to replace.

Boomers are loyal.

Even if a Boomer does not agree with you, she will do all she can to make the department and her team a success. She will not abandon you when she gets tired, bored, or distracted. She will stay and help you finish a project when everyone else has gone. She rarely looks out only for herself; rather, she looks out for the team and the company. If she does leave to take another job, she will be scrupulous about giving notice and in trying to time her departure so it is an auspicious time for the team. She will leave projects in good shape.

✓ *Management lesson learned:* Use the passion your older workers have for loyalty to help train and transfer knowledge to new employees. Expertise and information accumulated through their tenure is valuable, and Boomers love the teaching role. Also, stability is rare and will probably not be found to this degree in your younger workers. Since companies are constantly making changes and younger workers are concentrating on making their next career move, is the loyalty and stability of the older worker worth your investment? You can bet that some of your customers who have had to endure multiple changes in account reps would tell you there is marketable value in long-term employees who help you reduce turnover. Customers whose businesses are large or complex are tired of retraining new representatives to handle their accounts. High account rep turnover is often a reason customers switch vendors. And internal stakeholders desire the same stability.

Boomers have a long-term view of most everything.
A Boomer is likely to look just as carefully at the retirement benefits and the health insurance a position offers as the salary. They are not "live-for-the-moment" folks. They look at potential risks and obligations in the future, and largely base decisions on preparing for these possibilities. This may seem like negative thinking to you, but preparing for worst-case scenarios is not all bad. Whereas a job that has become unchallenging probably wouldn't hold a younger worker, a Boomer might stick with it because of the tuition assistance it can offer her children or for the generous contributions to her 401K plan. Boomers always have their eyes on the future.

✓ *Management lesson learned:* As much as possible, try to figure out the long-term benefits of any changes you want to implement. If a Boomer can see the change as an investment, he is more likely to support it. Also, if you have budget or benefit cuts, try to find ways to offset the current cuts with some long-term benefits.

Boomers are more risk averse than younger workers.
Just as their long-term view holds Boomers in jobs that are no longer exciting to them, so does their cautious approach to risk. Although this generation has demonstrated that they can handle more big changes than any generation in history, small changes annoy them. They do not enter into change lightly or without much consideration. They have seen manufacturing fall on hard times; they have seen people leave good jobs for high-paying dot-com technology jobs that were quickly lost; and they are currently seeing their peers who changed jobs frequently facing retirement with little more than social security to support them. Change is not necessarily attractive to Boomers and for good reasons, based on their experiences.

✓ *Management lesson learned:* Tell your Boomer employee that you want her to be your transitional advisor. Ask her if you can use her as a sounding board and advisor when changes arise. Express how you value her opinion and her understanding of the risks and rewards of any change. Emphasize that the changes will probably take place anyway, but that her assessment of possible obstacles in the change process will be helpful to you in overcoming those obstacles. Be sure she understands that her role is not just to focus on the obstacles and problems but on solutions as well. Her emphasis in this advisory capacity should be on finding the most efficient way to thrive under challenging circumstances rather than defining and rehearsing the obstacles. This approach allows the Boomer to be vocal and open, yet it channels her energy into being a problem-solver instead of a problem maker.

Parents of Boomers were deeply affected by the Great Depression and many behaviors and fears trickled down.

These are "waste not want not" people. These are "eat everything on your plate" people. These are people whose parents saved and reused brown paper bags for wrapping. Fear of not having enough in the previous generation has led to the Boomer generation's tendency to hold onto things they should get rid of. They hold on to old paper files, they hold on to old ways of doing things, and they hold on to old equipment and software.

✓ *Management lesson learned:* If you see resistance to change, be sensitive that you may be tapping into some latent fears and insecurities. Ask how you can help. In your enthusiasm for "out with the old and in with the new," don't go too fast and scare these people. They are reasonable and cooperative. Most managers responding to the XYBoom Survey agree that Boomers are willing to learn new technologies and techniques, and that the manager simply needs to give them a bit more time for the learning curve. Approach them in a way that is supportive and ask their advice about the best way to implement changes, even if the changes must be done in stages.

Accomplishment is the Holy Grail to most Boomers.

Have you ever been pushed by your parents to go for a goal that was more theirs than yours: a more prestigious college, dean's list, a job with a larger company, or a graduate degree? If so, you know how accomplishment can be almost like a religion for some people.

The Baby Boomer generation is all about accomplishment. This almost Puritan ethic thing they have going is, to them, the only way they can morally and ethically feel they are doing the right thing. In a Boomer's mind, he must at all times be able to say, "I am giving my best and working as hard and as long as I can to accomplish my goals. I must not fail to accomplish the objectives set out for me. I will succeed and not disappoint my manager or let down the company." Do you hear how many *I*, *me*, and *my* words are in those statements?

Yes, the accountability within the Boomer generation is to be admired and even learned from. Their focus has been on individual accomplishment and made sayings like "stand on your own two feet" so ingrained in the Boomer belief system that some have a hard time changing to the concept of team accomplishment and getting work done through collaboration. The Boomers were the first generation to be given the keys to success by working through organizational levels, climbing the corporate ladder, and playing the game—all the traditional elements of success. And for the majority of their careers, the strategy has been to accomplish all they can individually. Many successful Boomers would even tell you that part of the fun in their rise to success was in beating out the competition, who happened to be their friends and coworkers.

✓ *Management lesson learned:* Be sure to tie some of the Boomer's performance goals to team efforts. Also, remind older workers of the expertise they can leverage from others through questions such as, "Have you talked to Jason about your marketing in New Caledonia? I think he had a project there."

Older workers have high expectations of themselves and others.

Boomers may have been idealistic in thinking that their world would always be better tomorrow, but for the most part their thinking was accurate. Because the Boomers really believed that tomorrow was going to offer them great new opportunities, they were always preparing for that success through self-improvement books and training. These high expectations that Boomers have of themselves cause them to demand optimum performance from everyone else as well.

Boomer Translations

A Boomer Would Say	Gen-Xer or Gen-Yer Would Say
Stand on your own two feet	Two heads are better than one; four are even better
The buck stops here	Sharing goals means sharing accountability
If it is to be, it is up to me	If it is to be, it is up to the team
Lead, follow, or get out of my way	Let's all go on this adventure together and see where the path leads us; we may find new information that redirects our goal
Business success is built on hard work and rugged individualism	Whatever
We must forge ahead	Why? Tell me about the reasons for all this forging before we invest ourselves in it
The power of one	It takes a village

✓ *Management lesson learned:* Work with older employees to be more accepting of varying work styles and approaches to getting work done. Develop the Boomer's appreciation of the contributions of each person on the team. Design project teams that require the Boomer to depend on others more.

Boomers are not as quick to plug into teamwork as younger workers.

Because of a strong work ethic, high expectations of others, and a tendency to be evaluative, they are not as open to working as a group, whereas younger workers have done school and work projects in teams for their entire lives. For Boomers, teamwork is a learned behavior and does not occur naturally in their lives. It's not that they are averse to team participation; it's just that they see most tasks as individual responsibilities.

✓ *Management lesson learned:* The exciting thing is that once you teach a Boomer the benefits of approaching projects as a team, they usually love this approach. It is difficult at first to get Boomers to ask for help because they feel that asking is a shortcoming. However, once you show them how to leverage the strengths of everyone on the team (especially their own), they feel immense relief at not shouldering so much responsibility.

Boomers are strong on personal accountability.

The upside of Boomers being so driven and single-focused is that they really have a strong sense of personal accountability. To see projects through to closure, no one beats a Boomer.

✓ *Management lesson learned:* As Boomers are retiring, many companies are seeing a decline in personal accountability, so you may need to keep this in mind when hiring. Actively recruit for this quality. Also consider including this trait in performance evaluations in an effort to strengthen accountability in younger workers.

Different Expectations on Day One of a New Job

Boomers: Began their careers expecting to work for the same company until the end of their careers

Generation X: Had mixed expectations upon starting careers; eventually, even those stalwartly loyal to one company became resigned to the probability of job changes in their futures

Generation Y: Has no expectation or desire to stay with the same company; multiple job changes are in their future and they are excited about it

Boomers' work style and communication may be more formal than yours.

Because grammar and structured formal writing were far more important to the Boomer's early career, they often speak, write, and act with more formality than you are used to. This is normal behavior for a Boomer and not an affectation. They expect everything from meetings to conversations to have a bit more structure.

✓ *Management lessons learned:* Try to meet the Boomer halfway on these expectations, especially during the time when a Boomer is forming his first impression of you as a professional. Also, don't slip into slang or other behaviors that may seem unprofessional or exclusionary as you are forming a trusting relationship with your new employees. From time to time, tell the older worker he has permission to be less formal with you so that you can gradually transform the workplace.

Boomers like technology but are not as excited or infatuated by new products as you may be.

Watch a Generation Y employee's response when he hears there is a new technology coming out. A Gen-Yer will rush to consume the newest and best, and celebrate new versions and explore the expanded utilities. Generation Y and, to some extent, Generation X have been brought up in the era of:

- What is the newest, slimmest cell phone I can get and how fast can I add my friends and other information so I can use all the features?
- I have an Xbox but the new Xbox is coming out and the graphics are supposed to be insane, so I am sitting on the edge of my seat to get my hands on the new version. I don't even consider that there might be a learning curve or that it will require set-up time, because I will breeze through that.

This attitude of running as fast as you can toward any new technology is so different from the attitudes of most older workers. And yes, like you, I have a fifty-something relative who is a rabid online gamer and a technology hog, but she is the exception and not the rule. The diversity among the Boomer generation has been widely documented, and nowhere is the range of diversity greater than when considering their approach to technology. The range goes from the ridiculously out of touch to the sublimely skilled. Still, most older workers do not, as a group, go running headlong toward a change in technology. Fewer of their generation stand in line the night before Microsoft or Apple releases a new product. And at work, that means they are not as excited about changes in software, hardware, or anything technologically related. Chapter 4 is entirely devoted to this key differentiator between older and younger workers.

✓ *Management lesson learned:* Don't let the apparent lack of enthusiasm for new technology make you lose faith in the older worker. They may not be in love with the technology, but they want to learn it. These survivalist employees will do what it takes to adapt if you approach them with consideration and a staged approach.

Boomers may have tunnel vision.

When working on projects, they forget to slow down and be sensitive to people groups, environmental issues, or other factors not directly related to their responsibilities. In general, Boomers are not as outwardly focused on issues like these as on the work itself.

Of members of Generation Y who are employed on a full-time basis, 79% said they want to work for a company that cares about how it affects or contributes to society.

—"The 2006 Cone Millennial Cause Study: The Millennial Generation: Pro-Social and Empowered to Change the World"

✓ *Management lesson learned:* Boomers are good people who lead by example to demonstrate inclusiveness. When you review plans and projects, ask questions about people groups, the environment, and important stakeholders. Slowly build sensitivity to these issues by asking questions about them early in a project. Model concern and sensitivity as you integrate these issues into everyday work tasks and processes.

Family time and work-life balance may not be as much of a priority to Boomers as to younger generations.
Though Boomers value family life as much, they believe the way to demonstrate caring is by providing security and things. Older workers are generally generous to their families, especially when it comes to providing educations and other aid that will help their children get a better start in life. Still, you will see some judgmental looks if you walk away from a demanding project because you want to spend the evening with family or work out to maintain your health. To most Boomers, the work comes first and the family should understand. And a healthy lifestyle is very low on the priority list of the older worker if there is a time crunch at work.

According to the article "Generation and Gender in the Workplace," by Families and Work Institute, Generation X and Y are described as more "family-centric," or "dualcentric" (with equal priorities on both career and family) and less "workcentric" (putting higher priority on their job than family) in comparison to Baby Boomers. Fifty percent of Generation Y workers valued family time more than work, while 41 percent of Baby Boomers did.

✓ *Management lesson learned:* Provide clear communication about schedules and expectations, especially when work gets behind. Be sure that your older workers are not risking burnout because they are neglecting their health or their families to catch up a project. Be especially careful not to dump the deadline crisis on an older worker who will be sure to finish up while your younger employees are spending time with family or at the gym. Evenly distribute and schedule responsibilities during high-stress times.

There is an inherent attitude difference between the older and younger generations.

All of the above factors have led to attitudes that are, at times, polar opposites between older and younger workers. Here are just a few of these attitudinal differences:

A Boomer Would Say	Gen-X or Gen-Y Manager Would Say
It's the right thing to do	Who decides this "right" way? Whose moral compass are we using? Is it a fit for all the moral codes represented in this work group? Is it a fit for me?
Everyone knows that it's true	Does everyone include all races, ethnicities, genders, lifestyles, and ages?
TWWDT = The Way We Do Things	Maybe it's time to try a new way. I would like to create something unique and creative and not rubberstamp the old way.
Don't make waves; go with the flow; don't rock the boat	I would like to put my personal stamp on any project I undertake. Let's rock.
If management had wanted me to do it that way, they would have told me	I prefer thinking through new approaches to projects than being told what to do
We have always done it that way; if it's not broken why fix it?	If something has been done the same way for a long time it must be outdated. Let's try something new and innovative.

The following may or may not be true of any individual Boomer. Remember to assess each Boomer individually. They are the most diverse group in history. However, chances are, you will have less trouble when managing Boomers with these issues:

- Clock watching
- Work ethic
- Quitting
- Office politics
- Gaffes

And you will have more trouble when managing Boomers with these issues:

- Diversity
- Change and flexibility
- Technology

Boomers tend to be defined by their jobs. An older worker may define himself as inherently a Manager of Telecommunications at Koch whereas you may feel you are an environmentally aware family man who happens to work at Koch.

✓ *Management lesson learned:* Drawing identity from a job, especially a job held for a long time, is fraught with dangers. When change comes, not just the Boomer's job is threatened but his very identity. Understand that this identity threat will fuel emotions when you talk to the older employee about changes, especially ones that will involve a role or title change for him. Move slowly. Be an advocate and partner in aiding him in making any change successful. Come to meetings about change prepared with tangible resources and options to make the change successful for the older worker. They want concrete how-tos and not just encouragement.

Different Generations, Different Expectations

Generation X has been called the "me" generation but Generation "Y" takes "me" to the next level, in stereo and neon lights. Generation Y has been supported by their parents in their belief that they are special. Compared to earlier generations, parents have also provided almost instant gratification of the things their children desired. Because of the enabling attitude of their parents, Generations X and Y have developed some foundational beliefs about how the workplace should work. These attitudes differ dramatically from the older generation.

Starting on the first day of work, most younger employees have much higher expectations regarding how interesting and important the work that they are given should be. Although everyone desires interesting work, the Boomer's expectations are not as high as Xers and Yers.

Boomers Don't Expect:
- To stroll into the boss's office (or the boss's boss's office) and offer new ideas regarding how to run the business better
- To see you slow down a project in order to ensure that everyone is participating in the decision-making
- To have fun at work

✓ *Management lesson learned:* Fun and interactivity keeps younger employees engaged and coming to work. Not so Boomers. Though some older employees may get a kick from activities like these, most will see such antics as distracting and unprofessional. Let the Boomers play a role in planning and implementing the activity to build their buy-in.

In Conclusion

The most important thing to remember is that older workers are like all workers: you have to learn about each one individually. There is no archetypal Boomer employee. Just as you differ greatly from so many people in your age group, so do they. This compilation of generalizations about older workers is simply to give you some insights into the evolution of your Boomer employee. It helps to know where someone has come from in order to get to know why he is as he is now. Employees from the Baby Boom generation are probably even more diverse than from other generations since their generation span is longer and so much change occurred in their lifetime. Be sensitive to the issues discussed in this chapter but by all means prepare to be surprised and delighted by the variety of styles you will encounter from the Boomer group.

CHAPTER 2

The XYBoom Survey—Finding Out What Younger Managers Really Think about Managing Older Workers

Have you ever wondered if other young managers were facing the same challenges in managing older workers that you are? More importantly, would you find it helpful to know what they are doing that actually works? If so, the information in this chapter will introduce you to a survey that asks the hard questions of more than 550 Generation X and Generation Y managers like you.

In January 2008, I conducted a survey of Generation X and Y managers and supervisors who are currently managing older workers. I wanted to go directly to the source and find out about the challenges the Gen-XYers were having, the most effective solutions they had discovered, the advice they would give other younger managers, and information that could make you more successful. The instrument created was the XYBoom Survey. The results are a credit to both the young managers who are leading with such a lack of prejudice and to the Boomers who have been proactively supportive of their younger managers. The positive results that follow from the XYBoom Survey would not have been possible if all the generations, Generations X, Y, and Boomer, had not been open to accepting the differences, the gifts, and the feedback of the others.

These results attest to the value of diversity. In the survey responses, each generation demonstrates that it genuinely values the benefits brought to the workplace by the other generations.

Problems? What Problems?

The first good news is that not only are younger managers successfully managing older workers, but these Generation XYers really like and respect their seasoned Boomer employees. Time after time when asked about problems with older workers, younger managers wrote in to say that they either didn't have problems, that they actually found the older workers better in some categories and wished they could hire more, or that the problems were brief and temporary, easily overcome after some initial development. Naturally, when a survey gives hundreds of people a chance to say anything they want, you may find one or two who have had bad experiences and have negative comments, like the lone respondent who simply said, "Old people suck." One might be tempted to toss such a random response; however, I think it is important to include for the very reason that negative responses like this were so rare.

Throughout the book, quotes from the responses to the XYBoom Survey are incorporated into the chapters. Younger managers are highly collaborative, and almost all of the respondents offered suggestions or advice to younger managers like you.

Before reading the management strategies, you may want to review the results from the objective section of the survey that follows.

Results from Generation X and Generation Y Respondents

Following are the objective results from the XYBoom Survey. Six questions were asked and Generation X and Y managers responded. The first five questions were objective, and the sixth question was open-ended. The answers, advice, and strategies from the open-ended questions are included at the ends of Chapters 3 through 9.

XYBoom Survey Results for All Respondents

1. The greatest challenge I find in managing older workers is:

A. Differences in our timing such as the pace of work, speed, slowness	26%
B. Differences in style such as formality and judging what is appropriate	23%
C. Differences in collaboration and working in teams	7%
D. Differences in use of technology	37%
E. Other	7%

2. The value I have found in managing older workers has been:

A. Learning from their experience and minimizing risks	27%
B. Different way of thinking about projects and ideas offering greater diversity of viewpoints	34%
C. Strengthening the organization and stability of the department and projects	16%
D. Product and subject matter knowledge	18%
E. Other	5%

3. The most effective way I have found to solve problems with older workers is:

A. Communicating face-to-face	69%
B. E-mail or other written communication	8%
C. Designing rewards, consequences, or other behavior modification approaches	8%
D. Taking a wait and see approach, not drawing attention to behaviors or comments	13%
E. Other	2%

4. If I could hire anyone I wanted for my team, I would:

A. Build my team with Generation X or Y employees and not hire more older workers	16%
B. Add even more older workers to my team	22%
C. Based on my experience, I have no preference between hiring older or younger workers	58%
D. Other	4%

5. Please check the box that best describes your age:

A. 1963–1979	90%
B. 1980–1987	9%
C. Other	1%

XYBoom Survey Results for
Generation X Respondents Only

1. The greatest challenge I find in managing older workers is:

A. Differences in our timing such as the pace of work, speed, slowness	27%
B. Differences in style such as formality and judging what is appropriate	23%
C. Differences in collaboration and working in teams	7%
D. Differences in use of technology	37%
E. Other	6%

2. The value I have found in managing older workers has been:

A. Learning from their experience and minimizing risks	27%
B. Different way of thinking about projects and ideas offering greater diversity of viewpoints	35%

C. Strengthening the organization and stability of the department and projects	16%
D. Product and subject matter knowledge	18%
E. Other	4%

3. The most effective way I have found to solve problems with older workers is:

A. Communicating face-to-face	71%
B. E-mail or other written communication	7%
C. Designing rewards, consequences, or other behavior modification approaches	7%
D. Taking a wait and see approach, not drawing attention to behaviors or comments	13%
E. Other	2%

4. If I could hire anyone I wanted for my team, I would:

A. Build my team with Generation X or Y employees and not hire more older workers	16%
B. Add even more older workers to my team	22%
C. Based on my experience, I have no preference between hiring older or younger workers	58%
D. Other	4%

5. Please check the box that best describes your age:

A. 1963–1979	100%
B. 1980–1987	0%
C. Other	0%

XYBoom Survey Results for
Generation Y Respondents Only

1. The greatest challenge I find in managing older workers is:

A. Differences in our timing such as the pace of work, speed, slowness	13%
B. Differences in style such as formality and judging what is appropriate	22%
C. Differences in collaboration and working in teams	14%
D. Differences in use of technology	40%
E. Other	11%

2. The value I have found in managing older workers has been:

A. Learning from their experience and minimizing risks	27%
B. Different way of thinking about projects and ideas offering greater diversity of viewpoints	31%
C. Strengthening the organization and stability of the department and projects	18%
D. Product and subject matter knowledge	15%
E. Other	9%

3. The most effective way I have found to solve problems with older workers is:

A. Communicating face-to-face	51%
B. E-mail or other written communication	15%
C. Designing rewards, consequences, or other behavior modification approaches	15%
D. Taking a wait and see approach, not drawing attention to behaviors or comments	14%
E. Other, please specify	5%

4. If I could hire anyone I wanted for my team, I would:

A. Build my team with Generation X or Y employees and not hire more older workers	15%
B. Add even more older workers to my team	24%
C. Based on my experience, I have no preference between hiring older or younger workers	56%
D. Other	5%

5. Please check the box that best describes your age:

A. 1963–1979	0%
B. 1980–1987	98%
C. Other	2%

Introduction to the Seven Gaps Every Generation X or Y Manager Must Bridge with Boomer Employees

Older workers have all the smarts, all the ability, and all the resources to accomplish anything a younger worker can. In addition, the older worker has an asset that only she has and that will take a younger manager years to accumulate—rich business experience. The XYBoom Survey, however, revealed some gaps you may have to bridge with an older employee before he can realize all that wonderful potential.

You Are What You Were Taught

You have not necessarily had a better education than your Boomer employees but it certainly has been different. The messages you have received about your own abilities and the world around you (as in the global world) are vastly different from what the Boomer's teachers and professors were telling

25

him. And let's not even go there about the differences in technological training you received as compared to the Boomers.

Again, you take for granted the rich learning opportunities you had all around you, even as a preschooler. You know those things you think everyone knows because all your peers know them? Well, the Boomers don't necessarily know all of those things.

This is an opportunity for you to demonstrate leadership in introducing older workers to new ways of thinking about a variety of workplace issues. You can teach them and lead them to become better employees and to better integrate into the workplace of today by bridging some gaps in their backgrounds.

Seven major gaps that exist between younger managers and their older workers that correspond with the following chapters are:

- **Gap 1:** The Time Warp: Older Workers Operate in a Different Time Zone from Generation X and Y
- **Gap 2:** The Great Divide: Technology
- **Gap 3:** Communication
- **Gap 4:** Managing, Developing, and Motivating Older Workers for High Performance
- **Gap 5:** Trust, Respect, Etiquette, and Office Politics: The 10 Ways You Shock Your Older Employees
- **Gap 6:** Managing Diversity in a Four-Generation Workplace
- **Gap 7:** Creativity, Innovation, Change, and Risk

Two Resources for Managing Each Gap

Do you want to look forward to going to work every day to manage those older workers? The secret is in managing these seven gaps that exist in the work styles and viewpoints of older workers and younger managers. Following every gap listed below are three resources to help you manage each situation successfully. First, you will find strategies derived from current best practices and an experienced management consultant. Following those recommendations are the ideas submitted by Generation X and Y managers through the XYBoom Survey. These real-time recommendations are from XYers who are facing the same challenges you face every day. The Dos and Don'ts at the end of each gap summarize the best advice from your peer managers and the experts.

Bridging the following gaps through the management strategies suggested will yield high-performing older workers, amazing results, and a genuine enthusiasm for seeing that older worker first thing in the morning.

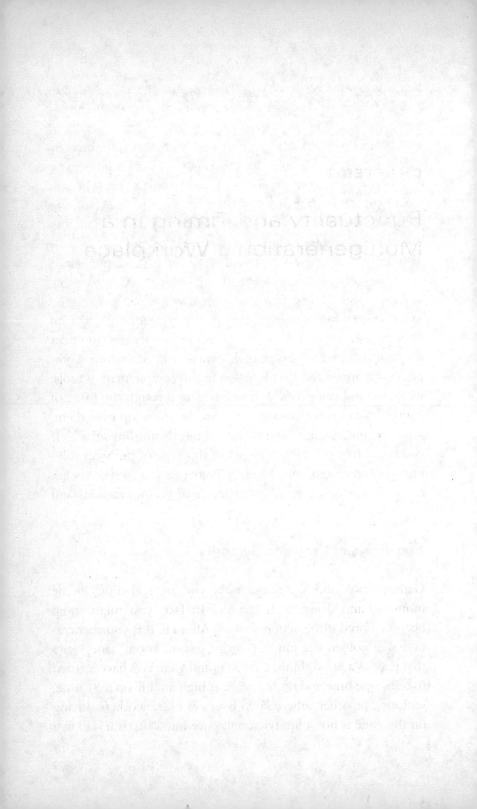

CHAPTER 3

Punctuality and Timing in a Multigenerational Workplace

Do you ever feel work seems like one big video game with opportunities and obstacles popping up moment by moment for you to deal with? From the moment you enter your workplace, you are on red alert to use your full complement of tools, weapons, and resources. As you navigate through the maze of your workday, some obstacles require you to jump over them, some require stealth, and some require a full-out attack. If you come to work fully engaged in this type of problem-solving, you are not alone. Most of your peers are experiencing the same rush and thriving in today's more spontaneous and unpredictable workplace.

Two Views of Time and Seniority

Generation X and Y managers like you are real time, in the moment, and down with change. In fact, you might even become bored if the action slowed. After all, it is your generation that coined the phrase "zoom, zoom, zoom" and views that pace as a good thing. Gen-Xers and Gen-Yers have learned to telescope time and do not place as high a value on lead-time, seniority, or other time-related issues as older workers. Living on the edge is not a lifestyle preference but a survival skill in a workplace experiencing a rapid rate of change. When you pull up to the office each day, you never know what next great thing upper management will throw your way, and you may secretly get a buzz from the challenge. Older workers may not find edginess so comfortable, nor may they have much appreciation for its value.

If you want to see a disparity between the viewpoints of younger and older managers, just sit on a hiring panel interview with a mixture of generations. In most cases, a Generation X or Y employee will value creativity, relational qualities, and recent results in a candidate over years of experience. For more than the obvious reasons, older generations value seniority and experience more. Great hiring decisions are made when the various generations collaborate and appreciate the values expressed by others.

To Be or Not to Be on Time

Even the word punctuality sounds old-fashioned and a bit up tight. Just as Bill Clinton pondered the meaning of being verbs, you may be saying, "What exactly do you mean when you say on time?" Older workers may believe in the saying "The only way to be sure you are not late is to be early." They are more likely to arrive excessively early for meetings in order to ensure they are on time. Not making mistakes is as important to these folks as risk-taking is to your generation. One risk most Generation X or Y managers feel quite comfortable taking is to arrive at meetings barely in time. Both generations see the other's approach as a time management deficiency.

Younger workers do not understand what the big deal is about being so focused on tasks being done synchronously at a specific time. The younger manager may be more focused on results than measuring what time the work began and ended. An older worker may judge his manager who always arrives justin-the-nick-of-time as having poor work habits. Conversely, younger managers may feel the older worker is a slacker if he has time to spend those extra minutes just sitting in a room waiting for a meeting to start. Today's mantra of doing more with less has been a constant in the work lives of Gen-XYers, so younger professionals are in their comfort zone with last-minute change and short-term planning. In fact, they revel in it. The X and Y generations are more flexible and fluid about start times. And today, since many meetings are canceled on short notice, some of that waiting may, in reality, be a waste of time.

Is an Employee a Slacker If He Always Arrives Early?

Does the sight of an older workers sitting idle in a conference room just waiting for an upcoming meeting make you slightly crazy? The visual of the older employee simply sitting alone in a room in order to prevent the remote possibility of being five minutes late sets off alarm bells when your job depends on achieving higher and higher performance levels from your team. But how do you manage these experienced senior workers who don't view their behavior as wasting time? And is being chronically early a performance issue at all?

Managing the Chronically Early

The disconnect between your generation and the older generation regarding time has some costly repercussions:

- Generates friction as both generations view the time habits of the other as detrimental to productivity
- Diminishes respect for certain team members of both generations
- In either case, wastes someone's time
- Leads to communication problems and can polarize a team along the lines of age

You must address time-related problems and communicate your expectations to the older worker or you may begin to see deterioration of performance among other team members. The strategies at the end of this chapter will aid you in addressing this time gap problem.

So how do you go about doing the retooling that must be done on both sides to bring forth the best performance from older employees?

How to Handle Hourly Employees and Individual Contributors

Justin Marsh is a thirty-five-year-old manager in a telecommunications firm. His department processes hundreds of applications for installation of service a day. His employee, Beverly Stratton, is always the first to arrive at his meetings. Her punctuality is not surprising since Beverly arrives fifteen to twenty minutes early to each meeting and then sits in the conference room waiting for the action to start. Beverly actually stops being productive several minutes before that; she says she does not want to begin processing an order in case it gets complicated and she can't break away from her computer for the meeting. Justin has hinted to Beverly that she should be so busy with order processing that she can't afford the luxury of just sitting there while her computer is idle. Beverly cheerfully tells him that the only way to avoid being late is to be early, part of the value system of "good employees" from earlier generations. Justin is becoming more frustrated each time he walks by the conference room and sees Beverly sitting idle long before the start of the meeting.

Potential Strategies

1. **Give Beverly a responsibility that will use her time in the empty room productively.** Assign her to place tent cards or set up the LCD projector. She might as well do something while she is in there by herself. Another use of her time would be to round up the perpetually late employees. It will be difficult for her to be early as she tries to herd these balky folks.

2. **Ask Beverly who she thinks the most productive employees in the office are.** Then ask her if she has ever noticed their arriving early to the meetings. Tell her that three months from now, you want to be able to name her as one of the most productive employees. Explain that the first step in doing that is to use every minute up to the time the meeting starts.

3. **On Beverly's performance plan, write the following goal:** Increase orders processed by arriving on time or no more than three minutes early for meetings.

4. **Give Beverly a card that says "Five Late to Meeting Passes."** Tell her that she has earned the right to enter a meeting late if she has been processing orders. She can be late up to five times in the next year with your blessing.

5. **The next time Beverly arrives fifteen minutes early for a meeting, be waiting in the conference room.** Say, "Beverly, I'd like to try an experiment. I don't really know how this will turn out but I am curious about something. Let's go back to your desk for just a minute." When you arrive at Beverly's desk, ask her, "If we did not have a meeting right now, which order would you be processing?" Then ask Beverly to start processing the order. If she is able to process the entire order prior to the meeting, then you have given her a dramatic example of how much more productive she could be. If she is half finished, show her how to pause and save that order to be finished later. Then ask her to do the math. If Beverly processes just one extra order a week, she will process at least forty-eight extra orders a year. How many days

does it take her to process forty-eight orders? If Beverly processes twenty-four orders a day, she will be taking two days of unpaid vacation time each year to sit in the conference room not processing. Explain to her that you cannot give her two extra days of vacation time a year but that you will give her an afternoon off if she can go ninety days without coming to a meeting more than three minutes early.

6. **As with all managerial problems, begin with open questions and positive communication and give the employee every opportunity to improve the situation before a formal plan is implemented.** Have you clearly stated what changes you want? Example: "Beverly, I would like to see you processing orders right up to three minutes before our meetings start. That means you cannot be in the conference room five minutes early. Can you make that happen?"

7. **Reward Beverly for being late.** For decades, Beverly was rewarded for being on time. She cannot "hear" Justin say that her excessive devotion to being precisely on time is not valuable to him. Instead, he wants that extra fifteen minutes of work. Beverly clearly wants to be a rule follower and do the right thing. Justin should sit down with her privately and say the following: "Beverly, I know you strive to do the right thing in every situation. What I need from you right now is every minute I can get from you to be used to process orders. In fact, I am going to reward you for every time you are late because processing an order makes you late to one of my meetings. If you are really packing in as much processing as you can, you will be late sometimes and I understand that. In fact, I am going to give you an extra break each time you are late due to processing an order just before a meeting."

8. **Consistently praise older, time-challenged employees for any evidence of improvement in areas related to managing time and resources.** Ruthlessly look for any vestige of improvement

so that you can begin a campaign to positively reinforce evidence of any of the following:

- Working up to the brink of a meeting or other stop time
- Improved performance
- Risk-taking related to timing

How to Handle Managing Professional and Managerial Employees

Justin also manages Ed, an engineer whose team takes twice the usual time to design solutions to installation problems. His solutions are usually perfect and he checks the work of his employees more thoroughly than his younger peers, but the rest of his peers feel he is not carrying his load. Justin has been looking at the Jobs Completed Report and has found that Ed's team completed 30 percent fewer designs than the most productive member of the management team. Justin needs to make sure Ed steps up his productivity before the other members start slacking off.

Potential Strategies
1. **Develop a chart showing the number of installations each team has accomplished over the last month.** Also include the number of reworked or faulty installations. Show Ed the visual representation of who accomplishes what but leave off names except for his. Then point to the chart showing the number of installations and tell him that the number of solutions installed will be the only barometer of success you will be using over the next quarter. Point to the rework and faulty installation column. State clearly that quality is not going to be the criteria used at all to evaluate success. Urge Ed to manage his team to work with speed and to free himself from looking backward. Sometimes

employees who were trained in slower-paced times need permission to make mistakes, something unheard of in earlier times.

2. **If Ed makes excuses and does not appear to be taking initiative to change, tell him you are going to do everything you can to help him get his numbers up.** First, show him a written performance plan with a specific number of installations his team must accomplish each month. Next, tell him that since he cannot find a solution to the problem, that you are going to get him some outside help. That help can include:

- A time management coach
- A former employee who can come back as a consultant to work with Ed to identify ways to improve his speed
- A time management course offered by your company, American Management Association, Career Track, a local university, or other source
- Shadowing the fastest manager for two days

3. **If you have a strong relationship with Ed, you could ask him,** "What concerns you most that requires all this double-checking that is slowing you down?" After he explains the issues, write them down on a sheet of paper. Then tell him that for the next ninety days you will take responsibility for any of the consequences he mentioned but that he has to step up his performance by 10 percent.

4. **Ask Ed if he has a strong team member whom he can charge with scheduling.** The team member can share some of the responsibility to make sure that the team is moving ahead on schedule, including time for Ed's checks. The move will be developmental for the employee as he is prepared for a supervisory role. Sometimes a partner can instill a sense of energy and pick up the pace on a more constant basis.

5. **Plan this meeting for a time when you have plenty of time to listen.** Older workers generally take longer to explain underlying reasons. Also, if you don't thoroughly listen, Ed will think it is your understanding that is lacking. Ask Ed to discuss his view of why his numbers are 30 percent lower than some team members (not mentioning names). After Ed completely details all his reasons and you listen with empathy, then say, "Those are reasons I can respect, but I cannot let those reasons prevent your team from designing as many installations as other managers' teams. I hope you understand that if I allow your low number to stand, others will lower their numbers and we will fail to meet what the company has hired us to do. What are some possible solutions that you can suggest for solving this dilemma, because it must be solved this month?"

Again, let Ed explain or complain, but be sure to listen respectfully. If he comes up with solutions and agrees to bring up his numbers, say, "I really felt that you were the one who could best help me deal with this. Thank you. Let's get back together in two weeks to see how your plan is working."

If Ed does not come forth with solutions and commitment, then give him three days to work on a plan for solving the problem. Set up an appointment for him to come back in three days with a plan. Tell him that no one knows his job as well as he does and that the best solutions would come from him. Stress to him that you do not expect his perfect installation record to stand. Urge him to take some risks.

6. **At the next meeting, your problem should be solved.** If not, create a chart for Ed that demands he ratchet up his performance gradually. For example, you may ask his team to design two extra installations this month, four extra installations next month, and so on until he is completing as many as his peers.

Long-Term Versus Short-Term Career Views

Do you realize what a value clash you have with older workers when you talk about your career and future? First, professors and mentors have taught you that part of your job is to look after your own career. Some older workers were never taught that. In fact, they were taught throughout most (maybe all) of their careers to be unselfish and never speak up for themselves or ask for promotions, raises, or developmental opportunities. They are holdovers from a paternalistic management structure in which promotions were given to them, almost as favors, and in which career development is something done to them, not for them. The executive or manager was like a benign dictator who would dole out perks or promotions rather than having a long-term development plan for each employee that would strengthen both the employee and the company. Asking for these perks and promotions was speaking out of turn and pretty audacious.

When you talk about the training you are seeking from the company so you can move ahead or when you are talking about the next department you want to work in to round out your company-wide experience, you are acting as a responsible professional. You are wise to consider what your next move is strategically so you can advance your career. Older workers, however, may view you as disloyal, ungrateful, and greedily ambitious. In their minds, you have broken "the rules" that "everyone" knew when they were building their careers.

Consider the background of the older worker who thinks you are trying to push too hard. According to Morris Massey in his book *What You Are Is Where You Were When*, most people form their values by the time they are eight years old. A fifty-eight-year-old worker was eight years old in 1958. That's the year the first domestic jet-airline passenger service was begun by National Airlines between New York City and Miami.

As you can see, the world was not moving too fast. People did not usually just jump on a jet and arrive somewhere quickly, even in the United States. If you wanted to go to see family in another state, there was a strong possibility that you would take the train, a rather leisurely form of travel. No one was routinely whipping out credit cards, except a Diners Club card, and that was almost exclusively at restaurants for the select few who had this prestigious card. So if you are unsympathetic to an older worker whose pace seems slower than yours, try to understand the context she comes from. To her, you are moving at warp speed.

In the older worker's view, you want things fast and easy. You may be perceived as unwilling to pay your dues. Your education or specialized expertise may have helped you leapfrog ahead of this worker. With the fear of shortages of younger managers due to the mass exodus of Boomer managers, you and your peers have often been fast-tracked. In doing so, you have taken a shortcut around something the older worker reveres more with each passing year: seniority.

According to Len Gainsford in his article in *HR Magazine*, the generation he calls "boomers" has a much longer-term view of careers than younger generations:

> *For a start, the term "career"'is associated with baby boomers. Generation X looks more to a series of work-related experiences interspersed with "lifestyle" events such as cross-cultural learnings. Generation Y employees begin and may stay with part-time employment. Generation Y sees the multischeduling of personal priorities and work experience as the expected state of affairs over a working life.*

If you really want to shock your older workers, tell them you are not really promoting a career but may instead "stay with a series of part-time jobs interspersed with lifestyle events and cross-cultural learnings!" This is career sacrilege to an older worker. But to younger generations, the modular approach to building a career may be practical. Diversity of experience and a willingness to change companies and even skill sets frequently may best equip you to stay afloat in volatile times. But this changeable approach to career planning has not been what senior workers have observed as universally successful in previous decades. Their experience, though dated, is very real.

A few of the bubbles you have seen burst in your lifetime have been the dot-com bubble, a couple of stock market freefalls, and the real estate/mortgage decline. If you or your family was touched by any of those industry events, you learned the necessity of having fallback plans and flexibility. Keeping your eye out for new opportunities and always having your résumé tuned up in case something appealing comes along is just good career management. Older workers, on the other hand, were brought up in the manufacturing era when goods, companies, and careers were more durable and long-lasting. Their fathers (not their mothers) may have worked for the same company for at least thirty years and got the gold watch and a pension (not the flighty and less trusted 401K). They never updated their résumés unless a dramatic change, a disastrous event, or an unexpected opportunity was thrust upon them. To these senior employees, you might appear to have one foot out the door and not really be invested in the job you have now. Be discreet about talking about your future career moves or your openness to new opportunities. You can save those conversations for your peers who are laying similar plans of their own.

Looking for the Next Big Thing

Another reason you are wise to be open to new opportunities is that the hot industries today may not be hot by the end of the year. What is on the horizon for your industry? For the marketplace in general? Today's managers and executives must be more visionary about their work and their careers to keep up with the fast rate of change. Markets and career strategies have been in a state of flux throughout the lives of Gen-Xers and Gen-Yers. To be successful today, a manager must be willing to change companies, learn new technologies and functions, and relocate if needed, sometimes internationally. Not so with workers from older generations whose markets and industries often took decades to change. Their definition of success was to move in as linear a path as possible, usually through only one or two companies. When workers changed jobs in the '50s and '60s, people asked what was wrong, either with the former company or the employee. Your generation is much faster about moving on for a variety of lifestyle reasons: to pursue a slightly better opportunity instead of waiting for an opportunity where you are, or for any number of reasons. Even when not actively interviewing, smart managers are always looking ahead at possibilities in case of downsizing and mergers.

Today, jobs are often awarded to younger managers like you because of technological expertise, international experience, or education, none of which are as valued by older workers. You, on the other hand, may have viewed some older workers as stuck in a comfortable place and unwilling or unable to adapt and move forward with the next big thing. The resulting chasm between the generations in their views of career movement has been the cause of much friction in the workplace. Have you experienced similar friction or resentment?

One strategy is to create development plans for all employees, particularly older ones. The plans should have opportunities for professional growth as well as promotions and traditional advances. Give them opportunities to update their skills, language fluency, and other marketable assets. If no movement forward is available at this time in your area, consider lateral moves and rotations. Chapter 5 offers greater detail on this type of development of older workers.

Development of Short-Timers

Unless the employee's retirement is iminent, career moves should be available to him. With the high turnover of younger employees, even short-timer older employees may offer the same length of tenure and should be given the same opportunities. The majority of younger Boomers responding to the XYBoom Survey did not see short-timers as a significant problem. Also, many Boomers are deciding at the last minute to delay retirement, and the short-timer may have more years left than he originally planned. Occasionally you will find a short-timer employee who truly does not want development. If the retirement date is within a year, you probably should accept the employee's decision. Beyond that, urge the employee to participate in his development. No one can be sure of the future. Ask Enron and Delta employees.

More can be found in Chapter 6 about developing and motivating employees.

Timing Is Everything

Synchronizing your sense of timing with your employee's timing is key to working effectively together. Acknowledging the value the older workers can bring from their view of time and blending that with today's need to live on the edge in the workplace can improve the performance of all generations.

Thoughts on Managing Different Attitudes to Time and Timing

The following are actual comments related to work pace and punctuality that were written in by respondents to the XYBoom Survey. Only a representative sample of answers is included.

- Older workers are often slower than their younger peers.
- Older workers tend to work slower, less efficiently.
- Older employees tend to work slower and use older techniques.
- Older employees are unable to adapt quickly, think outside the box.
- Personally I have no problems with older workers. I have seen younger managers who have less patience when dealing with older workers who are slower, or those who have been doing the job for many years though not the same way the younger ones would do it.
- I tend to do everything pretty fast and as a result I sometimes get frustrated. I find if I slow down a bit and communicate clearly things go much better.
- Some of them are slow, set in their ways, and stubborn. However, they are knowledgeable and reliable. You have to find the right balance. I also have learned to be flexible and let them work at their pace in their way when possible as long as I get the same results. Here I use the same philosophy that I use with my son: "Choose your battles."
- The pace of their assignment completion has been sometimes slower than their peers. Developing clear work plans has assisted in alleviating this issue.

Other young managers wrote in to say that the older employees are even stronger or at least equal to the younger workers in performance and issues of time.

- The older workers have a better work ethic and are more team oriented.
- The turnover rate for younger generation workers is a lot higher, so hiring older generation workers may have its advantages as well.

- My challenge is the same regardless of age, which is they all want the holidays off. I'm not able to do that.
- If I tell them what I would like to be done and why and listen to their input, they are much more likely to do what needs to be done. I also have learned to be flexible and let them work at their pace in their way when possible as long as I get the same results.
- Older workers are short-timers.
- Some of the older workers are winding down their careers and it is difficult to motivate them to take on new, challenging projects
- Dealing with limited career time spans
- They are so close to retirement that they do not put forth the same energy and effort.

Dos and Don'ts

Do slow down and communicate what you want clearly.

Do develop clear work plans with incremental deadlines.

Do keep in mind that the value older employees bring through lower turnover rates and dependability can offset a slower pace. Keep the total picture in mind before deciding an older worker's slowness is a management issue.

Don't have preconceived notions about short-timers or older workers. You may have the same types of problems with younger workers, so don't anticipate slow performance just because an employee is a Boomer.

Don't write off older workers who are close to retirement. If you treat them like they are history, you may be creating a self-fulfilling prophecy. You need to keep older workers fully engaged and feeling valued and rewarded until the very end of their careers. The team needs their productivity and they need to be needed. More and more, older workers are changing their minds at the last minute and postponing retirement.

CHAPTER 4

The Great Divide—Technology

Do you embrace diversity? Of course. You're no cretin from the dark ages. You've been schooled in diversity since first grade. So answer this question: Whom do you think will adapt to a new technology faster, an older employee or a Generation Y employee? Wasn't there just the tiniest part of you that wanted to make a snap judgment that the smart money would be on the younger employee?

Yet one of the unique things about what is called the Baby Boomer generation is its diversity. The differences in this population are as vast as the choice of ring tones for a cell phone. Nowhere is this diversity more profound than in the area of technology. After all, this is the generation that invented most of the technologies you think are so cool today. These technologies were on the drawing board years before they were options on your laptop or iPod.

In 1988, I conducted a seminar for the leading-edge scientists of BellSouth who shopped the world looking for new technologies to bring back to the Research and Development Department as possible new offerings from this telecommunications giant. Most of these scientists had PhDs in physics or electrical engineering or something that would enable them to discern if a technology might actually work on a large scale for their customers. One adventurous scientist might fly to Italy to visit a garage lab where a new invention was being tinkered with that might one day be the next big thing in cell phones. Or another might meet with a young inventor in Brazil who through experimenting with his home phones had found a new way to transmit pictures economically enough to consider this technology for individual consumer use. It takes years of study and development and debugging to ready these technologies for use, and you and I are the beneficiaries today of the technological imagination and creativity of many Baby Boomer techies. These BellSouth engineers and scientists were and are today as savvy as any Generation Y employee.

With that said, there are still Boomers who detest new technologies and wish we could go back to a simpler time. On days when I rack up scores of e-mails in my in box while I am in a meeting, I think they have a point. At any rate, the range of technical savvy and openness to changing technologies is broader in the Boomer generation than in any other generation in history. This diverse population is dramatically divided on the issue of technology.

In her well-researched article entitled "The Many Faces of the Baby Boomers" in *Christian Science Monitor*, Kim Campbell speaks to one of the greatest difficulties in approaching older workers, whether marketing to them or managing them. The very diversity of this generation that makes them strong and valuable in the workplace also makes a one-size-fits-all management approach dangerous:

> *An obvious example of diversity among the boomers is their age range, which spans 19 years and means that while some boomers are grandparents, others are still getting kids into preschool.*

The XYBoom Survey revealed some very encouraging news about the technical abilities of Boomers. Clearly, the data shows that there is a gap between the expertise and affinity for technology the Boomers have as compared with younger workers. The younger managers responding to the survey, however, wrote in time after time to say that after this initial learning curve that the Boomers could be counted on to learn and use the technology satisfactorily. The brief lag time in embracing the full robustness of new technologies did not appear to be an insurmountable management problem for most of the managers who volunteered comments.

Technical Diversity among Boomers

Technical diversity is most pronounced regarding the embracing of technology rather than the ability to understand technology. Some older workers are passionate about doing banking, bill paying, and communications online. Some are inventing new technologies as you read this. Many, however, do not embrace new technologies as readily as the Generation X and Y managers. Older workers are much more likely to be upset when they master a new CRM system, only to find that it is being replaced with an updated version which can do wheelies with customer information.

Contrasting Views of Technology among Gen-Xers and Gen-Yers

Contrast this to Generation X and Y employees. Generation X employees grew up as the Internet evolved and it was a fully functioning part of the workplace by the time they started their careers. The evolution was complete by the time the Gen-Yers were born. They never knew a time when e-mail, search engines, and text messaging were not part of an ordinary day. They look forward to each new incarnation of technologies for information and communication. They want the new stuff and dig in with both hands, er, thumbs, when upgrades come out.

The Great Technology Divide: Do You Crave Technology?

Boomers are likely to adapt to technology, get onboard with new technologies, and even desire to be more savvy about technology. The technology differentiator between the Boomers and Generations X and Y is that the younger generations think it's fun. Gen-XYers think getting a new computer system or software is a treat; they can't wait to try out all the bells and whistles. They consider it a fun afternoon to explore the new functionalities of Microsoft Word's latest version. To cap it off, they will be blogging, e-mailing, and text messaging for days with all their peers about what they like or don't like about what they tried.

A Boomer is much more likely to view learning yet another version of Word as a necessary evil, not arduous but annoying. After all, does it really do that much more? And is it worth the inevitable flaws that come with any new software? In any event, trying new technology can in no way be viewed as an item to put on the "Fun Things I Did This Week" list. A Gen-Xer would put it on that list and a Gen-Yer might be at the opening of the store on release date, eager to start the party early.

[T]hese young adults, born between 1977 and 1994, are slippery. They sucked down computer technology like Good Start formula from the day they were born—for no other generation in history is that true. As toddlers they watched MTV while sitting on their babysitter's lap; as children they searched the Internet for their science projects (and often taught their parents how to do the same); and in their early teens their backpacks had strap pockets for cell phones. By the time they entered junior high, many of them were text messaging under their desks in the same way earlier generations had passed notes (or learned American Sign Language, unbeknownst to

the teacher, as one of our editors and her peers did in the sixth grade). Now, as 18- to 29-year-olds out of the nest making their first major purchasing decisions, companies are scrambling to get their heads around what kind of buyers these new media-soaked, tech-rich people make.—Jessica Sebor, "Y Me: Members of Generation Y Were the First to Mature in a Media-saturated, Tech-savvy World—Here's How to Blow Past the Buzz and Get the Brand into Their Brains"

The "Waste Not, Want Not" Mentality of Boomers

Another difference between older workers and their younger managers is that the older workers tend to want to salvage everything and are slow to let go of processes and resources once acquired. They feel it is wasteful. Boomer employees are usually children of parents who experienced in some way the Great Depression. They saw their parents reuse wrapping paper and tin foil. They can't abide flagrant waste.

Now switch to your recent experience. How many times have you seen your company adopt a new technology or software, only to abandon it a year later?

The millions of dollars spent annually on hardware, software, training, and peripherals appear wasted to many Boomers. They feel something is terribly wrong. In many cases, they are right. In other cases, technology is improving so rapidly that the time and productivity savings of tossing out the old and adopting the new far outweighs the losses associated with the change. That willingness to change and charge off losses is a fairly recent accepted business practice. And Boomers have seen companies overextend themselves and fail, sometimes even facing criminal charges due to creative financing and bookkeeping. It helps to understand this concern over loss and waste, and to even consider the legitimacy of some of the senior workers' concerns.

Interestingly, both age groups believe in stewardship. Boomers want to save things, like old computers and old software. XYers are more global and want to save huge things—like the earth, clean water, and species.

Bridging the Technology Gap: The FACE Method

For all of the reasons explored thus far in this chapter, you may stereotype previous generations as being resistant to new technologies. How can you avoid being one of those prejudiced managers who think all Boomers think alike regarding technology? How can you effectively bridge the technology gap and make sure you are supporting and managing each of your diverse older employees in a way that is uniquely helpful to him or her? Take the four-step FACE approach when managing older workers to embrace and deploy new technology:

Face the fact that assuming you know an older worker's affinity and interest in technology based on her generation is as false as any other stereotyping. Would you make the same assumptions based on race or ethnicity? No. You probably would find this shocking. So be as open-minded in your take on things when dealing with an older worker. Be intentional about not stereotyping based on age.

Assess the older worker's abilities and progress related to a new technology. Assessing her understanding early and at short intervals will prevent you from making wrong assumptions and stereotypes. Start with simple tasks for the employee to do to demonstrate her grasp of a technology. Choose tasks that should position the employee for success. A series of successful attempts spurs any employee on to tackle more complex and challenging tasks.

Communication is the common denominator in any successful implementation of technology involving older workers; keep it open and informal during the technology learning process. Open-ended communication is best, as it allows the employee to tell you anything he has reservations about. Examples of open-ended questions include: "Any thoughts on this new technology?" "What would you tell someone else who is just starting to familiarize himself with this technology?" "How is that technology working for you?" Open-ended questions that encourage the older worker to bring to the surface any thoughts, positive or negative, will help you avoid quick and incorrect judgments.

Educate your older employees to be open to new technologies, to use full functionality, and to articulate their technology needs, skills, and questions. Individual coaching or very small groups are best for this type of learning. Often, a peer is the best coach since the communication flow and trust level are already established.

Taking Technology Education to a New Level for Older Workers

What is the best way to learn anything? To teach it, of course. Steven Covey in his corporate seminars for *Seven Habits of Highly Effective People* learned that having managers teach one of the habits was the most memorable way to have them learn the habits. Similarly, if you require an older worker to teach a coworker about technology, you develop your team in a number of ways:

- The older worker must study the technology actively in order to teach it. Learning can be passive but teaching is very active.

- By teaching the technology, the learning is reinforced when the older worker repeats the steps or features.
- Teaching will bolster the older worker's confidence in himself.
- The worker may feel as if you have more confidence in her in the technology area since you chose her to teach another worker. That confidence can increase performance.

Of course, you will have to find the right technology for the older worker to teach as well as the right student. Don't set up an employee to fail by giving him a task that is beyond his skill set. But if you have a new employee, ask an older worker to teach him the basics of your software, intranet, or other technologies. Or, send the older worker to a class on a software that not everyone knows and ask him to demonstrate what he learned one-on-one with another employee or two.

Technology and Customer Service

Does technology (A) diminish or (B) enhance customer service? The answer is "Both."

A secondary reason for resistance to new technologies is that older workers may feel that the pervasive use of technology has led to the diminishment of quality and customer service. In some cases, they are right. I once had a conversation with the top retail banking executive from a large super-regional bank. This bank was experiencing huge growth by buying up small-town banks everywhere and turning them into branches overnight. Suddenly, the small-town customers were able to take advantage of all the technology and services of the much larger bank. Information was available to customers in one phone call or one website visit that would have taken hours or even days in the past using the small bank's older technology. Still, the executive told me, in the minds of older clients, customer service was perceived as declining. He said, "I now tell the staff of the acquired bank exactly what to expect. I can guarantee that in the minds of customers, the level of customer service is going to go down after an acquisition. That is because most customers see customer service as calling Sally Ann at the local bank and asking her to look something up for them. They really prefer that Sally Ann do this, despite the fact that they can instantly access that information from their phone or computer without waiting until Sally Ann has time to get back to them. Sally Ann is customer service to these folks. Actually getting what they want is secondary."

More Strategies for Bridging the Gap

In what other ways can you bridge the technology gap? You will make older workers more comfortable by talking through the new technological changes ahead of time, training everyone involved, and building support for new technologies by helping workers clearly see the benefits. Describe those benefits in terms that are meaningful to them. Training older workers on technology may also have to be adapted for their generation. If they have not been brought up doing Boolean searches on the Internet or purchasing items online, they may need some fundamental skills training before doing tasks that the average nineteen-year-old learned in elementary school.

For example, if you are a manager in a property management company and feel your signage company is overcharging you, you might solve the problem in a couple of hours. You would probably use online tools and approaches such as the following:

- Develop a description of a typical sign, including dimensions, materials, and colors, then fill out online quote features at a variety of signage websites to secure fast, competitive bids—no meetings, callbacks, or lengthy paperwork.

- Narrow the list to two vendors and purchase online a sign from each to compare quality to your current signage.
- Ask for references from the most competitive bidder and check references online.

If you delegate this task to a senior employee who is not experienced in using search engines or in shopping online, allow for the possibility that these tasks, though simple, may take a bit longer. You probably have purchased items from eBay or Amazon or other popular online vendors. You can probably do these tasks quickly. The senior worker may also be an avid online shopper and researcher, but you cannot assume that. You must *assess, communicate,* and *educate,* according to the FACE method.

Full Functionality Is Not a Priority for Some Boomers

One area in which most Boomers differ from their younger counterparts is in fully exploring all the functionality of the technologies they own. What do you do when you purchase a new cell phone? Play with the features, right? Within twenty-four hours your favorite numbers and ring tones have been downloaded, you can work the camera, and you probably have experimented with every available feature. The majority of Boomers take a bit longer. And some features, such as the calendar, may sit unused for quite some time.

A Gen-X regional sales manager of a *Fortune* 100 company tells of purchasing BlackBerries for his fourteen sales managers. These are very busy professionals who have to deal with having tons of details and surprises thrown at them daily. The young regional manager saw that an electronic calendar was the only efficient solution to tracking all those commitments and surprises, so he made the investment in the BlackBerries in September. About half of the sales managers were Gen-XYers and about half were Boomers. In November, when supplies were ordered, almost all the Boomers placed an order for a paper calendar for the following year. Virtually none of the younger workers did, working solely off the BlackBerry's calendar. The BlackBerries were in use by the older workers, but not the full functionality.

Technology: A Fun Conversation or Not?

Both Generation X and Generation Y are much more conversational about their experiments and adventures in trying out new features and seeking new ways to cut the time it takes to perform tasks using the latest technology. I have observed my MBA and undergraduate business students prior to classes at Georgia State University collaboratively but unconsciously teaching one another about functionality. Their conversation is constantly about the newest features of the iPhone or Microsoft's newest Windows or whatever is the latest technology incarnation. They discuss technology features on their smartphones, PDAs, or online games the way Boomers discuss movies or television shows. Even if they all have similar experiences with a new technology, they just enjoy talking about it. Talking about technology is not nearly as interesting to most older workers. They're just not that into it.

Thoughts on Managing to Create Excitement about and Competence in Technology

The following are actual comments related to helping older employees fully embrace and exploit technology. All comments were written in by respondents to the XYBoom Survey. Only a representative sample of answers is included.

Generation X and Y managers had more to contribute on the topic of technology use (or lack thereof) by their older workers than on any other topic. Just as the number one ranked challenge on the objective section of the XYBoom Survey was technology, it was also the most popular topic under discussion on the open-ended question section. Here is what your fellow Gen-XY managers had to say on the topic.

- Some older workers fall behind in the use of technology because they are set in their ways and don't want to change. This is the belief held by some Generation X and Y managers regarding some, certainly not all, of their older workers.
- Sometimes it is hard to teach the older generation technology and you get very frustrated.
- The older workers feel they know exactly how everything should be done and do not ask the appropriate way to do something in the current company they work for.
- They don't like new technology and have a hard time adjusting to change.
- I sometimes lose patience when working/training on the computer because they can be so much slower with technology.
- Older workers have an unwillingness to learn new technology; they also have a know-it-all attitude, like they don't have to listen to you.
- Some older workers are not resistant to technology but are simply afraid or unconfident. (Gen-Xers were astute in making that discrimination.)
- Older employees are not able or don't want to learn new computer systems.
- Older workers seem to be more technology challenged. I have to show them computer skills younger workers already know.

- Technology is by far the most difficult challenge. Most people have kept up with this and have no problems, but there are a few that have no clue what they are doing and it nearly cripples them.
- They are easily flustered by technology and unwilling to try to adapt.

Gen-XY managers are meeting with great success when they approach the technology gap by training, coaching, or goal setting. The technology problem is a temporary one that can be overcome fairly quickly. Here are some thoughts on what it's like to succeed in teaching older employees to handle new technology.

- The only challenge I have had is training a staff person over sixty on how to use the computer. It took time—but now he is great!
- Most of the people that I have worked with are really excited about new technology; they just don't know enough about it. Given the time, they like to learn to use it.
- I had a hard time explaining new instant messaging at first, but then had no problems.
- Teaching the older employees how to use new technology was a struggle until they realized the efficiency of it.
- Most are willing to learn—but most have little or no experience with today's computer programs that are vital to working and gathering information.
- Teaching them new technology skills requires a lot more explanation and hands-on experiences than it does when dealing with younger workers who understand the skills almost immediately.

- The difference in computer skills has been a challenge; some aspects I am able to teach my older workers but some I just have to delegate to myself.
- I enjoy teaching others, so I don't mind spending the time to go over the technology piece of the job—that's usually the easiest to teach—and they have the skills necessary for the rest of the position.
- Essential to understanding older workers is appreciating their individuality. They have different levels of acceptance and familiarity with technology—influencing everything from communication preferences to work ability.
- The biggest challenge we face is trying to convince older employees of the advantages of technology. I believe many see the value, but they are intimidated and sometimes suffer from the thinking that you can't teach an old dog new tricks. We have found that if we tutor them, older employees begin to see it is not as hard as they thought and that there are real advantages to being more tech savvy. Some seem to complain more about having to do certain tasks or are hesitant to learn new things that involve computers.
- Older workers tend to have a longer learning curve, especially with new technology. I have had to devote additional training time and tutorials for these workers; however, I have been able to benefit from their vast work experiences. Younger managers need to understand what motivates the older worker and be sensitive to his/her needs. Young managers, can at times, demonstrate frustration.
- Although many of them never do get very fast with the computer, they do learn to use it when they have to, and do not mind admitting that they need help with computer problems. I have no preference between older and younger workers overall because every individual is different, and a good manager can find a way to work with them all.

- Older workers are hesitant with new technology but it's not a problem as long as they can write their own instructions and they get one-on-one training.
- The most difficult challenge so far seems to be the unwillingness of older workers to adapt and accept new ideas and technology. I find it helpful, though, to talk to them more often face-to-face and to understand their side of the story. After all, we still need them for their experiences and knowledge.

Dos and Don'ts

Do learn what motivates each individual and use those motivators to help the older workers embrace new technology.

Do give the older worker a bit more time in his learning curve.

Do prepare to do some hands-on, one-on-one training with your older worker.

Do communicate face-to-face with the older worker as you introduce new technology. Be available for support and answers to questions.

Do experiment with different learning styles; for example, allow the learner to write his own instructions. Or, if written instructions have failed, try to talk him through the steps to using a new technology.

Do read Chapter 6 for strategies for giving feedback.

Don't forget to explain the advantages of the new technology before introducing its use. Sometimes you must get buy-in before you get compliance.

Don't assume each older worker has the same problems with technology. Some are intimidated; some are not. Some are techno-phobic; some are not.

Don't get frustrated and impatient. Set up training times and conversations about technology when you are in a good frame of mind. Not a morning person? Work with technology issues with your Boomer employee in the afternoon. Got a deadline to meet? It is probably not a good day to stop and discuss technology with the older worker. Choose optimum time for both you and the older worker.

CHAPTER 5

Communication on Four Levels

Communication is such an all-encompassing and complex area of your management of older workers that this section has been broken down into two sections:

Section 1: *Three Communication Differentiators: Who You Are, What You Say, and How You Look*

Section 2: *New Forms of Communication: Texting, E-mail, Blogging, sScial Networks, and Instant Messaging*

Communication is probably the most important of the gaps to bridge since it affects all of the others. If you can master the communication gap, you will be successful in bridging all of the other gaps, so this section is key to successfully managing older employees.

Three Communication Differentiators: Who You Are, What You Say, and How You Look

In *Bowling Alone*, Robert D. Putnam makes some startling observations regarding how younger Americans do not invest as much time creating "official" groups or building social capital as past generations have done. Their socializing is much more free-form and spontaneous; it may not even be in person. He notes that over the last twenty-five years the following activities are in decline:

- Attending club meetings: 58 percent drop
- Family dinners: 43 percent drop
- Having friends over: 35 percent drop

So what are we doing instead? We are still communicating with our friends but we are doing it from the comfort of our bedrooms or while we are driving. We keep in touch wherever or whenever is most convenient and comfortable for us. Why work so hard over a dinner party and have all that cleanup before and after? If conversation with your friends is what you want, let your thumbs do the work. Text messages fly fast and frequently, particularly among Generation Y friends, and the messages are real time and stream of consciousness. Some could argue that this type of communication is more authentic since there is usually no effort to hold back or edit anything as the thoughts rocket from minds to keyboards.

What this on-the-go technology has done is make communication very self-centric. Implied in text messaging and e-mailing is the following underlying attitude:

I will communicate with you when I want, at my convenience, and in my bunny slippers if I choose. Unlike in conversation with its awkward pauses, if I don't want to respond to an e-mail or IM, I just won't respond and you can think I was in a meeting or whatever.

And I can pour my heart out to you, monopolize the conversation, and be completely self-centered because you cannot interrupt me. And you can't wind down the conversation if I have blathered on too long because even if you walk away from your computer or phone, I can keep blathering as long as my fingers have an ounce of strength in them.

At times, this style of typing into the Ethernet leads to talking at people. Boomers feel a sense of loss and miss what they call a "real conversation," one with both parties present. They feel younger employees, managers in particular, are not learning the delicate negotiation of "real conversation." Yes, some profound conversations do take place at times through IM and e-mail, but most of it is just the type of filler like the "yada-yada-yada" from *Seinfeld*. And although the screen in front of some people makes them more courageous to say things they would not say in a more intimate setting with a human in front of them, at times they say things they wish they had not said. And unlike in conversation where two people can sense when there is a perceptual difference, e-mail does not provide this rich source of communication clues. Also, e-mail leaves the transcript for both of you to see in perpetuity, not to mention risking having the information forwarded to any number of people. Yikes!

So although Generation Y is considered the relational generation and Generation X has similar communication patterns, the Boomers would disagree. What relational means to each generation differs. These differences manifest themselves in three ways that are like the ABCs of communication:

A. Generational orientation to communication (who you are)
B. Verbal style differences (what you say)
C. Nonverbal norms (how you look)

Who You Are

Orientation to communication differs by generation. If communication is truly a two-way process, then you need to know where your older employees think you are going wrong when you communicate. Perception is their reality. As the designated leader, it is up to you to take the first step to bridging the gap in your communication. The first common communication gap is in generational orientation, which refers to the quirks and traits a generation acquires based on the generation in which they grew up and developed their communication style. The following chart gives an overview of the most common gaps related to generational orientation to communication.

Communication Gap: You shock them with your brash expectations that you can communicate with executives at almost any level.

Why Boomers believe they are right: Boomers were taught not to speak unless spoken to by management a couple of levels above them. They adhered to this rule for good reason: they would have been fired! For the most part, executives demanded top-down communication and would have booted the Boomers for storming the executive offices with their ideas.

Communication Gap: Boomers are either amused or outraged by your belief that management genuinely wants to know what you think.

Why Boomers believe they are right: The Boomers were not brought up to place much commercial value on their own creativity and innovation—or to think about those topics at all. You were brought up to believe that you are unique, special, and have great ideas to contribute and that you should be proactive in voicing your ideas. Boomers were brought up to think that if they come up with a really great idea that someone in management has probably already thought of it and is dealing with it. They feel it is presumptuous to assume the idea has never been put forward before now.

Communication Gap: Closely related to the topics above is your generation's orientation to timing of communication. You believe you can make important contributions and make a meaningful difference now and see no reason to wait for things the Baby Boomers may have waited decades for. You might as well text that senior executive today to share your latest idea for improving the bottom line and to ask for more responsibility to implement it.

Why Boomers believe they are right: Boomers began their careers in a workplace that was strongly hierarchical. Much of the recognition and reward of that workplace was based on seniority and there was a comfortable quality to that, an unspoken promise that the Boomer's loyalty would be rewarded by their voices being heard in due time, after they had proven themselves. They paid their dues and worked their way up over a long period of time, earning the right to be heard. The shortage of talented young managers has put you in a much more advantageous position than your older workers. When you seem to demand attention be given to you during your first month on the job, the Boomer may have one of two responses: an overwhelming sense of the unfairness if you are rewarded or a diminishment of their respect for you and your ideas if you are not recognized and rewarded. Not fair, huh?

Communication Gap: Unlike you, titles and levels in the hierarchy greatly influence how the Boomer communicates

Why Boomers believe they are right: The higher up you are on the org chart, the more a Boomer will listen to your ideas and respect you. Your generation is less influenced by titles and levels. If you differ from an executive or a senior employee, you may plainly tell her that you disagree with something she said. To you, this is openness, candor, and the beginning of a productive dialogue that may lead to innovation and change. To a Boomer, you are violating one of the basic tenets of the workplace and demonstrating intentional and very personal disrespect. And just as this could lead to the Boomer's disrespect, you may also find their generation disingenuous for being so status conscious. You may feel a bit righteous over the fact that you speak the same way to the CEO as you would to an hourly worker. The Boomer thinks this is just rude.

What You Say

What does being relational mean to you? Does it mean steady and fairly constant staying in touch with your friends and perhaps your employees? Does it mean IMing, Twittering, and texting real time about current projects and events? This "checking-in" and staying in touch form of being relational is very important to younger managers. Boomers just don't get it.

Another set of values held by your generation seems at first to be polar opposites. First, your generation values consensus about everything from which movie to see to what your mission statement for a *Fortune* 500 company should be. Electronic communication has made gathering and tabulating information more manageable, so you can actually collaborate more effectively than in previous generations. Even individuals are conducting mini-surveys among friends to make social decisions like where to vacation or what the group thinks is the best choice of colleges. Zoomerang surveys are not just for business these days.

The value that seems at odds with collaboration is that your peers are very big on asynchronous communication. The brick-and-mortar meetings the Boomers are so fond of holding might once have seemed necessary. You may, however, envision a workplace in which it would never be necessary to have everyone in the same room at the same time. E-mail, text messaging, blogging, and IMing may even be a more efficient way to accomplish what is going on in your current meetings. And who cares what time of the day the information is shared, as long as it is shared effectively? Chapter 6's Management Communication discusses effective meetings more completely.

Generations X and Y's higher comfort level with asynchronous communication takes many forms and contrasts sharply with the lower comfort level of most Boomers. It is fine with you if your part of the conversation takes place at 9:00 a.m. on the East Coast and your friend's response occurs when he gets out of a meeting at 3:30 p.m. on the West Coast. Boomers are used to synched-up conversation—meetings with every project member in the room and conversations that are dynamic because the volley of conversation goes back and forth simultaneously. That feels like engagement to them.

Asynchronous communication feels less engaged and more impersonal to Boomers. They do not communicate as well or as effectively this way. It mystifies them why you would go to MySpace and communicate rather than have a "real" conversation.

Choose your times to use asynchronous communication. If you really want the ideas to flow and to get the best thinking from your Boomer employee, you may have to schedule face-to-face appointments or team meetings for those critical times.

Gen-XY's Version of Being Relational

Another way you are relational is that you want to bring your relationships into the workplace. You want to talk about or Facebook about your friends, families, and significant others; you want their needs to be taken into consideration during workload planning; and you want to experience openness and authentic interest from your coworkers. It is your hope that your workplace will recognize and embrace what is important to you, and that may sometimes blur the edges between your personal life and your work life. Take a page from the playbook Boomers referenced when they were first building their careers:

1. **Do not date anyone from work.**
2. **Do not discuss your personal life at work.** It's kind of like Vegas. What happens at home, stays at home.
3. **Do not bring up a personal reason for asking for anything, not salary increases, time off, or perks.** For example, do not tell your boss that you want the day off to spend some quality time with your children. Instead, say you are sick.
4. **Do not be honest during job interviews about any personal interests or needs you have.** For example, do not say that you left your last job because of their strict dress code or how hyper they got about your being thirty minutes late occasionally, so you were looking for a more relaxed business environment.
5. **Do not ask what the company can do for you; state what you can do for your company.** Do not ask to be developed or mentored. If the good fairy of paternalism smiles on you, you might get a mentor in ten or twenty years.

Inclusive Versus Exclusive

Finally, to Gen-XYers, relational means being inclusive. Your generations are sensitive about ensuring that everyone feels part of decisions, that all people have access to the same information, and that the ideas of people at the lowest strata of the wage scale are respected. Your generation is particularly conscientious about attending to the needs and viewpoints of the differently abled, the employees and customers with language barriers, and minorities. Relational, for you, has some very broad implications.

The Boomer's Version of Being Relational

While your version of being relational is very broad, the Boomer's version is extremely narrow. And I am not referring to that sketchy part of their youth when they were still part of a system that discriminated according to race and gender.

After all, the Boomers were the ones who changed all that. See Chapter 8 on diversity for a fuller exploration of that type of exclusiveness.

More germane to their verbal style is that Boomers judge the relational quality of a person based on what they experience one-on-one. They tend to be quick to assess whether you are respecting them and connecting with them, so here are some things they are looking for:

- Are you looking the Boomer in the eye when the two of you have conversations?
- Do you observe the courtesies expected by every generation before yours: Greeting the Boomer when you first see him, shaking hands firmly and energetically, making sure to say goodbye at the end of the day or a meeting, saying thank you for advice (solicited or unsolicited).
- Do you value their time by being prompt for appointments?
- Are you agreeable when they voice ideas or are you abrupt when you differ? In your enthusiasm to collaborate, do you ever cut them off? Do you spend time expressing what you value about what a Boomer says before you strike her idea down? Gen-XYers are so used to brainstorming sessions in college that emphasized moving quickly from one idea to the next that they may not realize that rejecting a Boomer's idea so quickly can feel like rejection of the person. Boomers may have made it through college without ever having done a team project or a brainstorming session.
- Do you express the desire for a long-term relationship with the older worker? Boomers are big on the long term and are focused on the future. They like to feel you are building something.
- Will you invest time and patience in a conversation that is long enough to feel satisfying and meaningful to them?

The characteristics above define being relational to the Boomer. It is fine if they don't hear from you for days at a time; in fact, they probably would prefer it. They would trade all those IMs you sent trying to stay connected for one good conversation that felt like good communication, as described in the previous list.

You may feel that you have communicated well with your Boomer employee, but is it rather that you have communicated often? They seek something different from you than your college roommate and your peers in the workplace. They desire a more in-depth conversation.

One manager interviewed said that Generation X and Y were more transactional in their conversations, just wanting to get in, get the relevant information, and get out of the conversation—much as one would pick off information from an instant message. This had proven to be profitable in some instances in the *Fortune* 500 company this senior manager was employed by, but problematic in others. The company was a major telecommunications giant, and having great working relationships with vendors of complex technologies was a must. At first, some Generation Y managers were so transactional that they were treating every negotiation like an eBay auction. The value in investing and preserving relationships with vendors who may not be the lowest priced had to be communicated to the younger managers. Many of the vendors vital to the stability of the company's networks were being treated like telemarketers, so the relationships had to be rebuilt.

Managing the Boomer's Expectations for Good Communication

You are probably thinking, "There is no way I have time to have in-depth conversations about everything I communicate to my Boomer employees." And you are right.

Again, success will come from investing some time on the front end of your relationship with the Boomer, with some occasional maintenance in the future.

At the outset of your relationship with the Boomer employee, sit down and have a long (thirty-minute minimum) conversation with him about your communication style. Be sure you follow everything on the list above.

A Study in Patience and Communication

Ahmed, twenty-seven years old, supervises Sue, a fifty-four-year-old national accounts representative for a large telecommunications company. He describes the communication gap he has with Sue this way:

> *I like Sue a lot, and I have a lot of respect for her knowledge of our customers and products. It just takes her so long to tell me something. Sometimes I just need to know the terms of a customer transaction and if I need to do anything to facilitate the transaction. Sue wants to tell me all the account background and the challenges that have usually been resolved at the point I am hearing about them.*
>
> *I've learned not to ask her about her sales right after a call. Better to ask in the early morning before she heads out to an appointment. It's working for me.*

Communication Stylin'

The greatest breakdown in communication occurs between Gen-XYers and Boomers over style differences. Here is the way you may view a Boomer's communication contrasted with the way he views his style.

You May Think the Boomer's Communication Style Is . . .	The Boomer Thinks His Style Is . . .
Long-winded, circuitous	Full and rich with the ability to express himself based on well-developed vocabulary
Vague, pointless	His is a generation of ideas and talking about ideas is great conversation
Focused on the past	Drawing from deep experience
So driven that he is ignoring some of the people and opportunities around him	Focused on a goal as he was taught to do
A waste of time	Adhering to the academic rule of tell them what you are about, to tell them tell them what you have to, then tell them what you just told them
Falsely polite	Genuinely courteous as all people should be if the workplace is to be pleasant and professional
Not focused on facts but on background information that is really a waste	Giving you context
Too formal	Appropriate for a college educated person

On the other hand, the Boomer feels there are aspects of your communication style that could use development:

The Boomer Thinks Your Communication Style Is . . .	A Gen-XY Manager Thinks Her Style Is . . .
Abrupt, terse, rude	Efficient
Lacking in context; task oriented to the point of disregarding the person you are communicating with	Streamlined by omitting extraneous details
Sloppy, full of errors or slang, inappropriate for the workplace	Informal enough to be effective and put the staff at ease
Difficult to understand since you don't fully explain what you are talking about	In the moment
Lacking in interpersonal skills	Highly relational based on how connected he is to so many people, knowing much about the details of their lives
Nonresponsive to direct questions, e-mails, and other overtures to communicate	Appropriate; why make up a response to something that requires no response—seems a little superficial
Disrespectful—it shows in your bored facial expressions and your lack of eye contact	Fine—This neediness for eye contact makes no sense. How can one have eye contact while multitasking? Stopping everything to connect eyes is counterproductive.

How to Deal

Just knowing these differences in viewpoints is helpful. Toning down behaviors you know are alienating to the Boomer, especially until you gain a comfortable flow of communication with her, is a good start. Incorporate some of the behaviors the Boomer finds reassuring: establish eye contact at the beginning of a conversation, respond to e-mails and direct questions, and for a brief period, indulge her in listening to a few of her long-winded explanations. After you meet her halfway for a while, you can then say to her that you hope you do not seem abrupt for the next few weeks but that you are going to be snowed under with the annual report or the year-end budget or something that sounds big. You have now prepared her to understand that for a while she will not be getting the type of communication she wants. You can gradually wean her from all that TLC during this period. She will know it is the work that is demanding and not that you are being disrespectful. Perhaps she should have known this all along.

Boomer Communication Tips

- Boomers are the "show me" generation, so use body language to communicate
- Speak in an open, direct style
- Answer questions thoroughly, and expect to be pressed for details
- Avoid controlling, manipulative language
- Present options to show flexibility in your thinking
- Use face-to-face or electronic communication to reach out to them

—Christine Zust, "Baby Boomer Leaders Face Challenges Communicating Across Generations"

Communication Strategies

Incorporate mutual respect and tradeoffs into your relationship. Yes, you are the manager and have lots to teach this older employee, but he will learn best if he feels he is teaching you as well. Invite him to be your advisor on a tactical approach to a longtime client or to coach you on how to present to your executives. In turn, teach him the technologies that will help him multitask like you do or teach him something from your expertise that is new to him.

Encourage more synchronous communication through technology. Work out a compromise with your Boomer employee. Tell her you are looking forward to more informal face-to-face sessions. Then ask her to use IM to communicate on a specific topic or project. Boomers are open to learning new things. If you limit your request to one project, the Boomer won't feel she has to adapt everything overnight. Remind her that you often let your IMs stack up until the end of the day. Set realistic expectations on both sides.

Be careful with humor. Boomers have not been brought up on irreverent humor like The Family Guy and the Simpsons. They often think your humor is mean-spirited or vulgar. Their humor also tends to be drier.

Be prepared to be successful. One of the things that is great about many Boomers is that they really want to have good relationships with younger managers. These employees have been through many changes and setbacks in their careers and will adapt amazingly well if given a chance. Go into your communication with them expecting to form a bond with a great employee and supportive colleague. Quite often, your expectations are self-fulfilling prophecies.

How You Look

John Thill and Courtland Bovee's book *Excellence in Business Communication* breaks down the concept of low-context versus high-context cultures for managers attempting to communicate with people from diverse cultures and generations. Low-context cultures are extremely literal, basing communication on contracts and straightforward conversations. Germany and the United States are good examples of low-context cultures. High-context cultures like Italy convey most of their meanings through nuances, particularly nonverbal nuances.

Boomers are much more sensitive to nonverbal cues and other communication signals that come from the context of a conversation. They seem to have highly evolved antennae to pick up on meaning. The debate is whether nonverbal communication is a reliable way to exchange communication. Even if one person is very good at reading nonverbal communication, we all vary in how we express things nonverbally. For the most part, nonverbal communication is highly unreliable.

One person can be conveying interest with his facial expression and his listener might read that as confusion or negative concern. For example, a manager can be expressing surprise over learning some new and important information in a presentation. The employee, however, can read the look as alarm that he has done the wrong thing. And another employee who did not sleep the night before because he was up with a crying baby could appear to be bored, angry, or hostile, depending on the baggage of the listener.

Unreliable but Powerful: Nonverbal Communication

In short, nonverbal communication should not be as important to Boomers as it is, given its high degree of unreliability. It is, however, the most powerful part of communication to this generation. Surveys vary, but most state that between 85 and

93 percent of a speaker's message is conveyed through nonverbal communication. So all that content sent through e-mails and IMs was not nearly as powerful as how you looked when the Boomer told you how the project was going.

Mixed Message? You Lose

Think of the implications of how powerful your facial expressions are. Your relationship with your Boomer employees hinges on nonverbal communication. That means that if you are verbally telling an employee that his work is fine, but your face is betraying that you are actually disappointed, the Boomer will believe your face over your words almost every time. And your face may just look dispirited because you are hung over. Either way, the lack of strong, positive nonverbals has damaged the effectiveness of communication between your employee and you.

So just because you communicate frequently and profusely, that does not mean your Boomer employee thinks of you as a good communicator. One thing that technology diminishes is the personal touch, the feel and the response. To Boomers, your real meaning comes from the nonverbal cues—looks, touches, and gestures. All of this is lost in text messaging, e-mails, and blogs. Older employees may not even find you trustworthy if you depend on these vehicles for most communication. Because a Boomer can't get a "read" on you from an e-mail, he may feel insecure about your real meaning.

You may have had the experience of e-mailing information to an older employee that clearly states what you want done. Shortly thereafter, the employee approaches you and paraphrases the e-mail, asking you if that is what you want. Well, yeah. That is what you just e-mailed her. Why did she need to repeat this to you?

Because she needed to see you. She needed to see if you looked energized by this topic, urgent, negative, whatever.

Strategies for Communicating Nonverbally with Older Workers

Here are some strategies for demonstrating positive nonverbals for your older employees:

Balance every part of your body. If you are standing, your left shoulder should be balanced with your right shoulder, your left hip with your right hip, and your left knee with your right knee. If one side of your body is higher than the other, you don't look "on the level," like a "straight shooter" should. Likewise, when you are seated and talking to your older employees, sit up as if you are attentive to what they are saying.

Be sure to be expressive at some point during the conversation. Cock your head slightly to one side to show you are listening, look sympathetic, and show your approval nonverbally at all the appropriate times.

Mirroring is a great nonverbal technique. Mirroring is the practice of mimicking very subtly what the employee does. If the employee is very high energy and mobile, then you should be. If, however, the employee is downcast about something and very low energy, calm your movements. Sit in a posture that is similar to the employee's. Use similar facial expressions. It's kind of like dancing; follow the Boomer's lead.

The safest look is the smile. Smiles from managers to employees release endorphins, increase productivity, and improve work relationships. Practice smiling. Give each Boomer at least one smile a day. I know this sounds hokie but try it and you won't believe what an improvement you will see.

Eye contact is huge. You must connect with the Boomer's eyes or he will think you are either lying or totally lacking in self-confidence. Either one is bad for a manager.

Have You Thought about Your Voice Lately?

Just as nonverbals are not as highly developed by younger generations due to the widespread use of electronic communication, voice quality has also lost some of its vibrancy and expressiveness. Be sure to develop expressiveness in your voice. Learn to inject some energy when you are excited about launching a project. Learn to slow your rate and lower your pitch when you are trying to show how understanding you can be as you demonstrate empathy for an employee's difficult situation. Your voice is a complex musical instrument. Don't play just one note.

Be a Communication Triple Threat

Once you are sensitive to your Boomer's different generational orientation and you adapt your verbal and nonverbal style, you will see amazing results. Your Boomer employee will respond with higher performance and a more productive communication style herself. Over time, you will both influence one another and the gaps will narrow naturally, requiring much less effort on your part.

New Forms of Communication

Texting, e-mailing, blogging, social networks, and instant messaging are common practice for you. However, they are not so common, or easy, for your older employee. Here are ten things you are more likely to do than your older employee:

1. Develop your profile and post it on a social network site like Facebook.
2. Download music legally.
3. Download music illegally.
4. Share photos real time from a party or other event (though some Boomers are getting into this)

5. Instant message for personal communication.
6. Instant message as a more efficient way to get work done while protecting your time.
7. Customize your cell phone with unique ring tones, creative screens, and other features.
8. Create your own website for personal and social purposes.
9. Establish your own blog on a topic that interests you and generate a following.
10. Look down on another generation for not deploying technology to communicate more efficiently.

You may not have done all of the items above, but the likelihood that you have done any one of them is higher if you are Generation X or Y instead of a Boomer.

Generational differences in the communication mode of choice abound, and each generation thinks it has the best mix of technology and relationship skills. Generations X, Y, and Boomer each thinks it is the best at workplace communication.

You may shake your head in dismay (pity? condescension?) at the poverty of interpersonal and communication skills in persons of the older generation. Well, just know that they are making similar judgments about you.

Relational Communication: Personal or Technology-Enabled?

Each generation feels it is relational but for totally different reasons. Many of the reasons relate to whether one chooses to communicate by e-mail, blog, IM, text message, or face-to-face.

And each generation perceives that it's the other guy's communication limitations that are the problem. They feel that generationally, the others are lacking in something that will help them connect as communicators. How does this paradox work? How did it all start?

Pew and AOL surveys show that the number of IM users decreases with age. In the Pew report, 62% of Gen Y (age 18–27) who use the Internet are also IM users; 37% of Gen X (28–39); 33% of Trailing Boomers (age 40–49); 29% Leading Boomers (age 50–58); 25% matures (59–68) and 29% after work (age over 69).

—*Clayton M. Christensen, "IM Usage in the US"*

Generations X and Y: The Relational Generations

If you are between 19 and 43, you probably have read the hype on your generation, either X or Y. According to recent media, you are more relational than previous generations. If you are a Generation Y manager, you grew up staying in very close contact with your friends through text messaging.

Contrast this to the Boomers who often had to share one phone with an entire family and that phone may have been attached to the wall of their family's living room. What did this mean as far as communicating with their best buds?

First, the Boomers had to wait until they got home from school to make a phone call; that's right, no cell phones. Secondly, phone calls were usually supervised and sometimes even rationed by parents. There was no calling from the school bus and certainly no text messaging from the back of the classroom while the teacher was conducting algebra class. E-mail was nonexistent in those days. Whereas you are used to communicating real time and pretty much 24-7 with friends, Boomers feel a phone call or e-mail is more of an event, not as formal as an appointment but a bigger deal than the way you perceive it. To older workers, a business phone call or e-mail is meant to be well thought out, appropriately phrased, and observant of business etiquette.

The Evolution of E-mail Style

When e-mail came into the workplace, there were two schools of thought regarding how the content should be phrased. At first, only the super-techie geek Boomers had e-mail. Some literally built their own computers in order to participate in this new thing called the world wide web. Because this technologically elite group felt this Internet thing was like their secret passage of communication and they held the decoder rings, they felt secure in breaking all the writing rules and writing in a very stream-of-consciousness style. Their managers were not tech savvy enough to be on the Internet reading their correspondence, so the techies could relax and state things in an informal way they would never use in a letter or memo. (I know: What's a memo?)

In the early 1980s, companies began to use e-mail as their corporate communication tool to manage people and projects. Even nontechnical managers began to communicate via e-mail. They did not have any authorities to tell them "the Rules," and Boomers and Veterans are all about the rules and doing things right. By default, they adopted the writing rules for formal business correspondence. In some traditional college textbooks, you will still see this style recommended for e-mails. The salutation is "Dear Mr. Smith" and there may be a heading like a memo within the text.

Expectations of Older Workers Regarding E-Mails

Because of this history, Boomers still have a deeply ingrained expectation that an e-mail should be polite and businesslike in phrasing. Unlike the early days when few people in a company might ever access the Internet, today's e-mails must be grammatically correct since one never knows who will eventually receive a forwarded copy. And Boomers may expect a bit of a polite opening before being asked for information or a favor.

So what happens when, in your haste to get things done in the most efficient manner, you shoot off a one-line e-mail with no salutation, no opening acknowledgment, no capitalization, funky abbreviations, and no proofreading as evidenced by the many spelling and punctuation mistakes? Boomers do not regard the e-mail as professional and may eventually regard you in the same way. The perception of the Boomer is that you are a poor communicator and that you are careless and sloppy in execution.

Some Boomers may have dropped the "Dear" in the salutation and appear to be onboard with e-mail's more informal style, but there is still a long history of expectations in their minds that causes older workers to judge negatively e-mails sent by individuals, especially managers, who have not taken time to think through their phrasing and editing. Your peers may welcome the off-the-cuff, to-heck-with-traditional-spelling reckless style, but most Boomers do not. And they may not take the information and assignments as seriously if they think that you did not spend much time on the e-mail.

And by all means avoid using terms from instant messaging acronyms or other really cool but untraditional sources. One of the comments written in quite often on the XYBoom Survey was that Boomers and younger employees use different terms for things. For example, if you use ATM in an e-mail, you may be talking about what you are doing "at the moment," but the Boomer will be thinking of the cash dispenser at his bank. And if you finally teach your Boomer friend at work that when you say BFN that you mean "boyfriend," don't then confuse him when you also use BFN for "bye for now"; instead, use the more common B4N. Many Boomers are now familiar with many of the common acronyms for laughing like LOL for "laugh out loud"; however, they may not know all of them like CSL for "can't stop laughing." All this to say that using traditional language that everyone can understand is a common courtesy and just plain faster than trying to translate everything after the fact.

Gen-XY Style Is Unpremeditated and Authentic

Generations X and Y call their spontaneous, informal style of communicating relational because they believe it is more authentic. Whether text messaging, IMing, or e-mailing, a younger worker's emphasis is on these values:

- The message is more important than mechanics and writing style.
- The lack of thought put into phrasing content correctly is evidence of the authenticity and unvarnished honesty of the writer.
- Telling one's thoughts straight from the heart is relational.
- In the fast-paced workplace, this unpremeditated style is very efficient.
- An e-mail is informal but slightly more formal than an IM. An IM is a license to communicate like a caveman or a rapper. Don't use it if you can't take the language or the abuse thereof.
- Asynchronous communication rocks.

These values are strongly held by the majority of younger workers and rarely held by older workers; how do you bridge the divide?

Stefana Broadbent, an anthropologist who leads the User Adoption Lab at Swisscom, Switzerland's largest telecoms operator, has been looking at usage patterns associated with different communications technologies and concludes that people are in fact using different communications technologies in distinct and divergent ways. "The most fascinating discovery I've made this year is a flattening in voice communication and an increase in written channels," she says.

—*Tammy Erickson,*
"Do You Want a Date or a Quart of Milk? More on Texting"

E-Communication Techniques

In the early stages of your relationship with a Boomer employee, you should use the old "gradually turning up the heat on the lobster" style. In other words, you will have to devote just a bit more time initially to meeting the Boomer's expectations for correctness. After your first series of e-mails demonstrating that you can punctuate and that you do respect her enough to address her correctly in a salutation, you can begin to ease up and slowly adjust the Boomer to your more abbreviated style.

First, greet the older worker by using her name, at a minimum. A good rule of thumb is to greet the Boomer in a document in the same way that she greets you in order to establish mutual respect. If she greets you in an e-mail with "Dear Steve," then greet the worker with "Dear Jonathan." Consider the following two e-mails in which this policy was not observed. A Boomer employee e-mails his younger manager and states:

Dear Steve,

Will you be needing the materials plan for Project 809 by Wednesday? I had planned to turn it in by close of business Thursday until I saw your new project schedule with the Wednesday due date.

Sincerely,

Jonathan

The younger manager receiving this thinks this is just about transmitting information. He forgets it is about people and deals only with the necessary information. His reply is one line:

Send the project plan Wednesday.

Fast, efficient, and lethal to the manager-Boomer relationship.

To the Boomer employee, this terseness is not viewed as efficiency but as rudeness. No regard or even acknowledgment is shown for him as a person. His name is not even used. To the Boomer, this is the e-mail version of saying, "Hey, you."

Another misunderstanding of "the Rules" in this exchange is that the Boomer's e-mail is not forthright and direct about what he is really saying. His real underlying message is that he does not want to have to turn in the materials plan until Thursday and he is asking for another day. He clearly understands that, yes, Steve wants the plan on Wednesday. When Steve gives him the information-only one-liner, Jonathan's underlying message and feelings are disregarded.

What could Steve have done differently? Much of the miscommunication between both generations has to do with respect. Respect and regard must be clearly demonstrated or Boomers can misread signals. To convey his regard for Jonathan's feelings and message, Steve could have simply written:

Dear Jonathan,

It would be helpful to me to have the plan by Wednesday. Is this do-able for you?

Regards,

Steve

In this e-mail, the Boomer is greeted, he is respectfully asked for his input, and the message has a polite closing. All is well in Boomer world. And note that the e-mail did not need to be long to satisfy Boomer expectations.

How Often Should You Be Communicating?

If you are a Gen-Yer, you may be text messaging and IMing pretty frequently. As you are meeting about a project, you may be simultaneously text messaging others involved. As the meeting takes place and each participant speaks, your project is evolving, you are delegating via texting or IMing. This is progress, real time.

To a Boomer, this incessant stream of communication is overkill. It is also extremely distracting to a Boomer to be talking to you and seeing your thumbs flying at the same time. Your behavior is beyond inattentive to the Boomer; it is insulting to him and seems to diminish the importance of what he is saying.

Texting and IMing are not integral to the communication DNA of Boomers. A Boomer manager told me about taking a younger employee with him to furnish building materials to the City of New Orleans in the immediate aftermath of Hurricane Katrina. He allowed this younger employee to drive the truck to the worksite to help supervise the unloading of the donated materials. He tells of a hair-raising ride through the bayous and over high bridges as the twenty-something employee drove the truck while simultaneously text messaging her boyfriend and best friends nonstop about every new sight on this, her first trip to Louisiana. Her eyes were more on her BlackBerry than on the road and she was typing faster than he can type on his keyboard at home. She was perfectly comfortable with this multitasking. He was not.

Boomers were brought up in a time when a weekly phone call home from college or to out–of-state relatives was considered frequent communication. For many, "the Sunday phone call" was a very big family event. Why Sunday? Because the expensive long-distance rates were discounted on Sundays. There was only one phone company, so there had been no competitive reasons to offer free long distance or even low-cost long distance. Many families looked forward to Sundays to talk to grandma or other extended family.

For similar financial reasons, business long-distance calls were tracked more carefully and employees were discouraged from using the phone any more than necessary. Most of those restrictions are now gone from your workplace. The sense that a phone call is something to pay attention to, however, is still hardwired into a Boomer employee. They expect phone calls to be returned and they expect, well, phone calls. They sometimes prefer conversation instead of just a text or e-mail message.

In his article "Are Your Managers Ready for Generation Y," John Bishop asserts:

> *Generation Y or the "Internet Generation" will dramatically change every aspect of your business in the next five years. Change will be constant, rapid and revolutionary. Want proof?*
>
> *First, the Massachusetts Institute of Technology is putting all of their 1,500 courses on the Internet. They will be absolutely FREE to everyone in the world.*
>
> *A person will not receive a credit or college degree, but they will receive the knowledge. MIT believes that the "dissemination*

of knowledge and information can open new doors to the power-
ful benefits of education for humanity around the world." That
means students, educators and self-learners will be able to audit
these courses when and where they want.

Second, Bob Lutz, General Motors Vice Chairman, has a
blog, http://fastlane.gmblogs.com, to communicate directly
with his customers. It is an invaluable way to get important
information out to the market. It is also a vehicle for timely
and accurate feedback. Other GM executives are setting
up blogs to talk directly to and get information from their
employees. By comparison, Microsoft has over 1,500 customer
and employee blogs.

Third, YouTube is an Internet overnight success story. It
allows people to upload and share videos over the Internet.
To date they have 100 million videos on their site and receive
another 65,000 per day. The company was founded in Febru-
ary 2005, and was never profitable. Yet, Google understood
the potential of their technology and purchased the company
nineteen months later for $1.65 billion.

Choosing Your Communication Mode of Choice

Eric Mogelgaard of Cox Communications says that the average phone call lasts three and a half to four minutes. The average business phone call is five to seven minutes. The reason is
that in every business call is imbedded a personal call. Younger
employees like to skip the personal exchange of unnecessary
pleasantries and get to the message. That is why they use instant
messaging (IM). IMs can fly fast with no-frills communication,
which is precisely why you like them and precisely why Boomers think they are an abomination.

Mogelgaard also shared some insights into how stratified the
use of various communication technologies is across the various generations. From observations of Generations X, Y, and
Boomer, Generation Y is markedly higher in their use of instant

messaging. Generation X prefers e-mail even if they are savvy about messaging. Finally, Boomers use e-mail but also show the highest propensity of the three generations to want to meet face-to-face.

Your generation may also keep up a steady flow of e-mail and text messaging communication as a project management tool. This ongoing collaboration is part of the reason younger generations are perceived as more relational. Whereas a Boomer may wait until she has some substantial information together to form a more content laden e-mail, you see no reason not to forward information as it arrives on your screen. Because Boomers wait in order to organize and consider information more thoroughly, they may not communicate with you more than once a day—or even once a week. You may think these days of silence are uncollaborative, but the Boomers are not even aware they have gone dark for what seems like a long time.

Boomers see the influx of stray e-mails related to the project as disorganized and inefficient. They are more about getting all the information under control. And all the open boxes of unanswered IMs on a Gen-XYer's screen would drive a Boomer crazy. You, however, know what a rush it is to go back at your convenience and pick them off one by one in monosyllabic answers, if they require an answer at all. After all, unlike the Boomers, you do not put unrealistic expectations on yourself to answer every communication or to gather all the information on a subject before taking action.

The Information Explosion Changed Everything

And there lies one of the greatest differences in Boomers and Generations X and Y. You have grown up googling for information on products, homework assignments, and even that weird guy that just moved in down the street. You do not even start with the expectation that you can get all the information on a project totally under control, and you are comfortable with that level of ambiguity. Here are a few reasons your generation does not waste as much energy on control issues:

1. **You know you can't read the 284,000 Internet articles available on your project.** You use your team to absorb what you can and then go forward. Boomers, on the other hand, grew up being able to research and read everything on a given topic because it was all contained in a card catalogue—a very limited media for retaining information. They learned their work ethic prior to the information explosion and sometimes have unreasonable expectations of thoroughness and knowing everything on a subject before moving. To you, this is analysis paralysis.

2. **You don't feel embarrassed by not exhausting yourself by nailing down all the information.** Why? Because overnight the information could change or the project could change or even be canceled. That is okay with younger workers who expect change, are not put off by change, and actually kind of like change. Flexibility is one of the characteristics of younger workers that make them resilient in this ever-changing business environment.

3. **On a more somber note related to change: You have seen your world, your safety, and even the marketplace change overnight on September 11, 2001.** You have seen the way you viewed your school and classmates change through events like the Columbine shootings. Your reality is that anything can change. And in the scheme of things, is adherence to an e-mail format really a big deal? Not in your world. Getting things done faster and with few frills is more important. After all, there are no promises about the future. Living in the present and getting the job done in the fastest way

possible is more important than trading on value in the future or observing rules of the past.

Just keep in mind that the attitudes above are very specific to your generation. These are your reasons and they do not relate to the Boomers. Their reality was established for decades before the events above occurred. Although Boomers acknowledge these events, they were not shaped by them. Long-held values of older workers were not altered.

A Jupiter Media Metrix study found the time spent using instant messaging applications at work has been doubling instant messaging use at home.

—*Michael Pastore,*
"Instant Messaging Has Gone to Work"

Boomers Are Avoiding Instant Messaging

As more Generation Y employees enter the work force, this is just one of the communication technology gaps that will need to be bridged with the Boomers. For the most part, they are still relying on e-mail and, as stated previously, still show a strong preference for face-to-face communication compared to Generations X and Y.

According to the AP-AOL Instant-Messaging Trends Survey, nearly four in five (79 percent) at-work IM users say they have used instant messaging in the office to take care of personal matters; and 19 percent of IM users say they send more instant messages than e-mails to their coworkers and colleagues.

Why Boomers Don't IM as Much

And there are other reasons Boomers don't think instant messaging may be the best choice for the workplace.

First, they don't like the idea of having to sign up for yet another application or vendor, and perhaps needing several more like MSN, AOL, Yahoo, and so on. To a Boomer, a commitment is a commitment. They have gone from a world where there was one phone company and one phone number for everyone to a world in which they have to make multiple decisions about choosing vendors and signing contracts to get better deals. And they have been burned at times. They would much prefer not to get started with another mode of telecommunication at all, but when you tell them they will need multiple vendors for instant messaging their eyes glaze over and they lose interest.

Second, the Boomers feel deep in their bones that instant messaging is more a social media than a workplace media. They have a point. Consider recent research brought to light in Clayton M. Christensen's article, "IM Usage in the US":

Activities carried out using IM are fundamentally social. They include keeping in touch, coordinating evenings and weekends, playing games, dating and sharing of information. On this latter activity, Pew/comScore Media Metrix found that 31% IM users share links to websites or articles; 30% share photos or documents; 14% share streamed web content or video and 5% music or video files.

Third, instant messaging is part of the multitasking that Generations X and Y love dearly. To a Boomer, too much multitasking is distracting and could affect the quality of the work. Older workers see their younger managers instant messaging while simultaneously doing other work and think the manager is only giving the project half attention. Boomers were brought up to do one thing at a time and to give projects their undi-vided attention. That is just not the world of the Generation X or Y manager.

The majority of IM users browse, play games, talk on the phone, or watch TV while they instant message. According to comScore Media Metrix, 32% of IM users always do something else on their computer, whereas 29% do so some of the time; 20% always do something else off their computer, whereas 30% do so some of the time.

—*Clayton M. Christensen, "IM Usage in the US"*

Viruses and Security

Another reason your Boomer employee may be hesitant to add instant messaging to his communication repertoire is all the attention given in recent years to the viruses and other security threats that IMs can bring into a network. Are these valid Boomer concerns about IM? Consider this excerpt from a press release sent out by Akonix Systems, a leading IM security firm:

[I]ts IM Security Center (www.imsecuritycenter.com) researchers tracked 20 malicious code attacks over IM net-works during the month of July. This brings the total number of threats during 2007 to 226, a 78% increase over the same time period last year.

Similarly, Boomers are concerned about hackers, a growing problem with IM. As noted by Jack M. Germain in his article

"IM at Work, Part 1: Idle Chatter, Serious Risk," there is a definite danger to using instant messaging services:

> *Instant messaging applications are easy targets for hackers taking advantage of vulnerabilities. It is critical for businesses to pay attention to their employees' use of instant messaging during work hours, warn security pros.*
>
> *Failure to safeguard sensitive company data could expose corporate networks to intrusions from a growing variety of attack malware.*

How to Invite Older Workers to the World of IM

Addressing older employees' concerns about issues like this is important. Your generation is pretty philosophical about the inevitability of getting a virus somewhere sometime, but this is scary stuff to a security conscious older worker. Concede that she has a valid concern. Then point out that similar threats exist with e-mail and that if barriers like that had stopped e-mail that the workplace would not be nearly as efficient. If you want the team to use IM, ask the Boomer to use it on a trial basis. Give her lots of help in the beginning.

Similarly, you may want to share some of the more recent research about the concerns the older worker has about instant messaging, like that found in R. K. Garrett and J. K. Danziger's article, "IM = Interruption Management? Instant Messaging and Disruption in the Workplace":

> *In sum, our study of computer-using workers indicates that instant messaging in the workplace simultaneously promotes more frequent communications and reduces interruptions. We have argued that this occurs because workers are using IM technology to manage interruptions, postponing work-related communications until they are more relevant or less disruptive, and integrating communication with friends and*

family into the ebbs and flows of work. In some instances, work-related instant messaging also enhances employees' interactions with colleagues by offering an efficient mode of rapid communication and information exchange.

Explain to the older worker how IM improves your time management because you can:

- Time when you respond to questions and interruptions by putting messages aside
- Write abrupt, short responses because that style is accepted in IMs
- Answer a stack of IMs quickly while talking on the phone and, yes, multitasking

Text Messaging

Virtually everything stated above for instant messaging can be said about text messaging times two. For the sake of avoiding redundancy, the information won't be repeated, but beware. If you think Boomers think you are goofing off when you IM, your credibility may take an even greater dive when you are texting on your phone while at work.

Interestingly, however, Boomers are warming up to texting but not for work reasons. Their children, some of whom are your age, are texting and these involved parents don't want to be left out of the communication loop. Sometimes Johnny, who is off at school, won't make a call but for some reason will text Mom back.

Still, texting is still considered more a social not business application. Teach the Boomer to communicate with you on one issue via text if it is important to you. Knowing that the texting required is limited may make the task less onerous for the Boomer.

Blogging and Social Networks

Most older workers don't see the great efficiencies in blogging and the use of social networks. Because you don't have to update a zillion people individually by e-mail, these tools can be highly efficient.

Here are some strategies for engaging the older worker in blogging or using a social network:

1. For your next annual meeting, require each employee to participate in an internal network. All communication for the meeting, from invitations to reservations, will take place on the network.

2. As a premeeting or pretraining session icebreaker, require each employee to set up a blog on your intranet. The topic should be one of interest to the employee and can be about anything: fishing, modern art, a business topic, or anything the employee likes to talk about.

3. Ask the employee to find three blogs on topics related to your business. Maybe once he sees the application he will want to find more applications he can create. Microsoft is an easy and almost universal place to start.

Be Results-Oriented

The most important thing is to be aware and respect differences related to these communication channels. If your employee is achieving high performance and feels strongly about not using one or more of the channels, perhaps that is the right choice for him. Keep in mind your final goal and don't let your desire to update his skills inadvertently harm the Boomer's performance.

Thoughts on Developing Great Communication with Older Workers

The following are actual comments related to communication that were written in by respondents to the XYBoom Survey. Only a representative sample of answers is included.

- Communication challenges are more an issue of differences rather than conflict or problems.
- Communication styles are different; words do not have the same meanings.
- More than anything, basic communication of terms is important.

As you'll see, younger managers stated more solutions to communication differences than they did problems—very encouraging and proactive!

- Let them help with the solutions—make it their idea and it will work!
- It's sometimes hard to relate to older workers under me and hard to break in especially when they tend to band together. I find it helps to try and foster friendships with them. Going to lunch sometimes, away from work, to get them talking to me helps get them to be more open in the workplace.
- Take your time to explain things; treat everyone as an individual and reassure the vitality of the team communication.
- Older workers like to talk things out face-to-face, while younger employees appreciate an e-mail to bring up problems.
- Many times they have a very hard time relating to the younger workers and the younger workers feel that the

older ones are a bit too "parental" when dealing with them. I have had to step in and talk to both of them and point out the problems and ask them to communicate better and see the positives in the different perspectives that they both bring to the table.

- There was an employee who found it difficult to take advice on a project from a younger boss. This person thought he had more experience and knew it all. We had to come to an understanding that I had listened to his ideas but that the team was working in another direction. I encouraged communication in a brainstorming session and several ideas were brought up. Then it was my responsibility to make a decision and manage the project going forward.

- I just let workers know what jobs are coming up, so they know what to expect ahead of time.

- I provide constructive feedback that they value.

- Try to look at the situation from their point of view and use empathy to break down barriers. Don't exclude or presume based upon stereotypes.

- Older workers like you to be direct but respect their knowledge; they like you to explain why things are being done in particular ways rather than just asking them to do something a certain way without offering an explanation. An explanation helps minimize some of the communication issues.

- Being the authority is sometimes a challenge if there is a disagreement about a direction to take with the department. I try to always take everyone's opinion under consideration and try to make the decisions as a team. I don't always choose my way, but do change my mind sometimes based on the team's input.

- It's difficult because I often get labeled as "immature" in the business especially seeing as I haven't been doing it as long as some of the others. I have to prove that I know what I'm doing and that I am great at what I do on a regular basis. I just take things day by day and with an abundance of face-to-face communication, and we get through it. I also stay away from relating to the gals as their daughter. I've found that if I do relate to them as my mothers, they are more likely to quickly become upset with me like their own children. I also keep certain aspects of my "outside work" life completely to myself!

- Older workers have a different way to rationalize issues, and I have found it enlightening. Open communication has brought a lot of knowledge and experience in my particular field of work.

- Older people feel that because they are older, they necessarily know more. But in this day and age of technology, this may not be the case. I feel that the best way is to openly discuss things with the person being managed. Involve them in the decision-making process so they feel they have a say in the choices being made. I always keep in mind that there is more than one way to perform a job. I hear them out and try to take their advice, and possibly mesh the different methods to create a new way that would be beneficial and productive in time.

Dos and Don'ts

Do engage in collaborative decision-making and involving older workers in the process. If you have something coming up that is difficult for them, they will be much more cooperative if they were in on early discussions and contributed to the solution. Give them some control over the process and their work lives.

Do know what is important to them and acknowledge and reward them with that.

Do break up cliques and get your older workers offsite, perhaps at lunch with you, to build stronger one-on-one communication.

Do invest in lots of face-to-face communication; even if it is not your preference, it is probably the preference of the older workers.

Do seek the other person's perspective, whether you are managing a conflict with the older worker or helping your older worker with a peer relationship. Demonstrate how acknowledging and understanding perceptual differences can contribute to better communication.

Do show older workers that your ultimate solution is a blend of your ideas and theirs.

Don't get sucked into the management vortex of treating older workers as parents. It is easy for them to get parental and easy for you to diminish your authority and effectiveness in the role of the child. Treating an older worker with respect is different from allowing him to treat you like a child.

Do read Chapter 6, which contains ideas for more formal management communication such as performance appraisals and meetings.

CHAPTER 6

Motivating Older Workers for High Performance

Successful managers achieve employee motivation and development through two ways. One is through effectively directing the performance of older workers. The other is through precise management communication opportunities—meetings, career development, feedback, and performance appraisals.

Effectively Directing the Performance of Older Workers

Before we get into some serious strategies for motivating older workers, would you like to experience a Julia Roberts moment? I have some good news for younger managers. Your Boomer employees like you. They really like you.

So you are starting with an advantage. You have employees who are predisposed to want to do what you ask. They are more receptive to you than anyone ever predicted. They are open to receiving direction and leadership from Generation X and Y and think you are awfully good at your job. This is despite the fact that all kinds of dire predictions had abounded before 2000 as human resource planning experts prepared the workplace to have four generations working alongside one another for the first time in history. Instead, statistics show that older workers are fair in the way they judge younger managers and supervisors. You can count on being evaluated on your merits, and the good news is that younger leaders are faring quite well when evaluated by Boomers. The highest incident of unsolicited feedback received on the XYBoom Survey was that Gen-XY managers really enjoyed working with their Boomer employees, often preferring them to younger workers.

Given that you are in a great starting position, what are some approaches to use when you are faced with motivating older workers to achieve increasingly challenging levels of performance?

The Families and Work Institute (FWI) investigated this area, using 2002 data from a large and representative sample of the US workforce, and found that older employees (over age 57) who have appreciably younger supervisors are more likely to feel that their supervisors are more competent, more supportive of their success on the job, and more responsive to their personal and family needs than younger employees (Gen-X and Boomers) who have substantially younger supervisors.

—*Frank Giancola,*
"The Generation Gap: More Myth than Reality"

Snapshot of a Boomer Employee's Motivators

According to Morris Massey, the godfather of managing generational differences, Boomers value the following:

- **Competition:** Boomers value peer competition and can be seen by others as being egocentric.
- **Change:** Boomers thrive on possibilities and constant change.
- **Hard Work:** Boomers started the "workaholic" trend. The difference between Traditionalists and Boomers is that Boomers value the hard work because they view it as necessary for moving to the next level of success while Traditionalists work hard because they feel that it is the right thing to do.
- **Success:** This generation is committed to climbing the ladder of success.
- **Body Language:** Boomers are the show-me generation and body language is important.
- **Teamwork:** This group embraces a team-based approach to business—they are eager to get rid of the command and control style of their Traditionalist predecessors.
- **Anti Rules and Regulations:** They don't appreciate rules for the sake of having rules and they will challenge the system.
- **Inclusion:** This generation will accept people on an equal basis as long as they can perform to their standards.
- **Will Fight for a Cause:** While they don't like problems, if you give them a cause they will fight for it.

Now you don't necessarily have to take that whole list as is. It is something you can build on and adapt to your management style and situation. Everything Massey observes is not inherently the case. As you probably noted, his point on Boomers, acceptance of change goes against some of the points made in this book and learned from the XYBoom Survey. Let's translate this list to some motivational strategies.

Boomer Trait	Motivational Recommendation
Competitiveness	If feasible for your other employees, set up intramural competitions for achieving performance goals and routine tasks
Strong work ethic	Count on these employees to provide early coverage for customers or duties since they usually are the first to arrive.
Loyal	Are you trying to reduce turnover in an area? Assign Boomers to customers or tasks that could use a stabilizing influence.
Desire for recognition	Assign Boomers to the "brand name" or prestigious accounts. Ask them to be the speaker, presenter, or figurehead representative at upper level or large meetings. They like this type of acknowledgment and affirmation.
Show me the money mentality	Boomers are into bonuses, overtime pay, and perks. Your generation—not so much—but it works with these folks.

Fight for a cause	Make work goals larger than a set of tasks. Interpret how the tasks lead to the greater good, offer a vision of a long-term achievement, or find a way to make the work support a cause.

Motivate Them as You Would Your Peers

Use all the motivational techniques you might use with your own age group with Boomers because they will probably respond. Recent studies are showing that Boomers are not so different from their younger coworkers when it comes to what motivates them, including a study completed by Towers Perrin in 2006.

What are some of the basic premises of motivating people, even older workers?

1. Given a choice of doing a job well or poorly, all people would rather end the workday on a successful note. Even if they don't particularly care what you think of them, they want to think well of themselves.

2. If an employee is not performing successfully, be sure to investigate all the factors before you decide the problem is motivation. Has the employee been correctly trained? If the training was in a classroom, would the answer be to give the employee more hands-on or experiential training? Is the problem that the employee needs better equipment or other resources? Only after much communication and investigation should you arrive at the conclusion that you have an unmotivated employee.

3. Tom Guthrie, vice president of operations for Cox Communications, has been successfully improving performance of individuals in IT roles for twenty years. He says

that shortly after joining an organization, he identifies employees whose performance mysteriously is just not what it should be. He often finds that no one has ever bothered to sit down and find out why an individual is underperforming. Quite often, the employee himself can reveal gaps of knowledge he is missing. Sometimes, just a bit of mentoring or coaching is needed.

4. Be sure the employee is capable of the job. Do not waste time motivating an employee who simply cannot do the job due to limitations, whether physical, educational, or experiential.

5. Once motivation has been identified as the cause of under-performance, spend some time identifying what the right motivators are for this employee. Each one is different.

Motivators: Different Strokes for Different Folks

- Bonuses, overtime, and other financial rewards
- Perks like great parking spaces and sports tickets
- Extra time off at lunch, at the end of the day, or during the holidays
- Peer reinforcement
- Long-term career investments
- Caring and community
- The right thing to do morally or socially
- Spiritual
- Flex-time
- Team activities
- Praise, acknowledgment, and awards
- Consequences
- Deadlines and pressure
- Fear of failure

Management Techniques: What Fuels the High-Performance Boomer Employee?

Through decades of being molded by parents, society, and previous managers, there are some forces at work that may make your Boomer employee unique. Evaluate whether you can tap into some of these qualities to incent the older worker to increase performance.

Accomplishment

Although Boomers are great team players and agree with decisions by consensus, at heart they are free agents. They feel morally impelled to compete to be the best. Being the best is as important to them as it was to their parents in school, business, politics, war, and industry. Competition was a positive factor in incenting older workers to do their best and they believe in it.

Generation X and Y, however, may genuinely derive more pleasure from a team effort that all participated in and which really has no single star.

Likewise honors and awards may be considered cheesy to younger workers. After all, yours was the first generation whose little-league baseball coaches gave trophies to every single player just for being part of the team. Honors and awards are, therefore, less meaningful to you.

Be sure to find ways to acknowledge older workers in very tangible ways, even if you need to invent some awards for their accomplishments.

Strong leadership

Boomers like a bit stronger direction than younger employees, as verified by the XYBoom Survey. When you set performance goals, be stronger and more direct than you normally would. Boomers grew up in a workplace that thought command and control was the style of an effective leader. If you do not state goals and expectations clearly, Boomers may completely miss the point that you expect these goals to be met.

Kent Hawkins, assistant pastor of Mount Paran Church of God, an Atlanta megachurch, works with a large staff of leaders of all ages. He recently noted that the leadership books of the last few decades are all by highly directive and authoritative personalities telling other people how to lead in their command and control style. He is accurate in his observation that one rarely finds a manager with a collaborative style leading one of these seminars or telling others in a book how to manage. Fortunately, Generation X and Y managers realize the value of blending a variety of leadership and work styles; they even intentionally seek to hire diverse employees to balance their teams. Boomers, however, still expect a bit more of a top-down management style.

Accountability

On a positive note, you have a strong motivator in the Boomer's sense of accountability. When you give a Boomer a project and tell him he is in charge, he will go to extraordinary lengths not to fall short of your expectations or his, which may actually be higher. Be sure to tell the Boomer that the project is his baby and that he can lead it in his way since he is responsible. Be sure to give him the resources he needs to be successful. Setting a Boomer up to fail by not supporting him in his gut-busting approach to projects is just wrong.

The right thing to do

A strong motivator for many older employees is social and moral mores and norms that press them to do the right thing for the department, even if it means sacrifice for themselves. This generation wants their entire community to think as highly of them as possible and they do not want to fail to be standup human beings. You can be much more successful with an older employee than with a younger employee when you tell her this is the right thing to do.

Gratitude

All people respond to sincere gratitude, but older employees really flourish when you offer it. If you genuinely thank a Boomer for a job well done, especially if you do so publicly, you almost ensure he will continue to do whatever you praised him for. The one thing you must express thanks for, in order to motivate older employees, is their advice and the benefit of their experience.

The work they love

Be sure to allow employees to do some of the work they enjoy most. Everyone has parts of his job that he enjoys more than others. To keep an employee engaged, try to find parts of the job that interest him and integrate that type of work into his week.

Security

Helping a younger employee stay in a company or a department would not be a reward, but many older employees genuinely want to stay in the department where they feel most comfortable. Offering the employee more responsibility that might make her more indispensable to the department is a great motivator. Be careful with this one, however. No one can ensure that any employee or department can have tenure. There really is no such thing as guaranteed job security today.

The various generations differ in what they value in motivational strategies. Your generation is not as moved by plaques on the wall, awards, or gold watches as an older worker may be. In his book *Leadership Jazz*, Max DePree tells the following story of a leader confronting "new realities":

> *The owner of the company . . . would walk right into the plant, give a short speech to the first-year employee, and then produce a really beautiful symbol, the company's logo, on a sterling-silver tie tack, presented in a velvet box. One day the . . . young man opened the box . . . and said, "Gee, that's beautiful!" Then he calmly inserted it into the lobe of his left ear.*

Feedback

All employees need feedback but Boomers are not used to getting as much feedback as Generations X and Y. They may actually feel awkward if you give them frequent or elaborate compliments. That does not mean you shouldn't do it. It simply means that you may not get the same response that you would get from someone your own age. Your feedback is for the employee and not you, so don't judge its effectiveness based on what the Boomer says or does when you deliver it. See if his performance shows that the feedback affected him.

Remember that Boomers worked in an environment of zero to infrequent feedback. At some point during their careers, most companies (not all) began requiring managers to give yearly, and later twice yearly, feedback to each employee. Human resources would not have had to make this a required event if all managers were giving feedback anyway. Once the feedback was required, the quality of it was usually poor because managers were unfamiliar with the practice. You, on the other hand, have been brought up with intermittent feedback from teachers, coaches, managers, and parents on every aspect of your performance. It is normal and familiar to you, so you should be quite comfortable with it.

Just think of leaders who encouraged you or who strengthened your skills by comments they made. Pattern your style after managers you found effective, but adapt the style to your own personality. This authenticity makes you more credible.

Constructive feedback is difficult for younger managers to give to older workers. The style of younger workers is often more blunt and direct, so be sure to be polite and respectful as you begin the conversation. Do not dive in without positive preliminary conversation to soften the verbal blow.

A good model is the CARE model:

Compliment one thing the employee does well.

Ask the older worker if there is anything she thinks she could improve on. If the employee covers the performance problem you were going to address, skip to the next step.

Review the performance problem with the employee by giving an example or two from her recent performance.

Explain what she can do to improve and what you are willing to do to support her efforts to improve.

Remember that effective managers don't neglect positive or constructive feedback. People cannot improve performance if they do not know what they are doing incorrectly, so be sure to give accurate, descriptive feedback in a sensitive manner.

Find more challenging assignments to keep them interested. This is another motivational strategy that would be cheered and applauded by a Generation X or Y but should be handled carefully when approaching an older worker. The Boomer may be equally excited or he might view the request that he work on something more challenging as one of the following:

1. A prelude to being fired
2. A hint that he has not stepped up his performance or spiffed up his game in a while
3. A threat
4. A dreaded change that will require stupendous effort
5. An opportunity to fail

All of the above may seem ridiculous to you, but in the Boomer's long experience he has probably witnessed a time when each of these disasters occurred. Again, clear communication is key to finding out if the older employee needs a challenge.

Older generations may feel uncomfortable meeting Generation Y feedback expectations. Traditionalists favor a "boot camp" feedback approach in which "no news is good news." Boomers had to balance their own belief that more communication is better with the reticent communication style of their Traditionalist bosses, so they adopted the annual performance review with a file full of documentation. Generation X members generally give frequent feedback, but their straight talk can seem undiplomatic and blunt.

—Lee Ann H. Webster, "Sharpen Your Communication Skills"

And once you find out that the employee is up for a challenge, be sure to provide it. Older workers quite often get in a rut but are not as vocal as younger workers are about telling you that they are bored or want a change. Again, fear holds many back from saying they want a change. They do not want to be known as complainers and they may have concerns that the change they would experience would be much more sweeping than what they actually want. These security conscious employees tend to suffer their boredom in silence, which usually affects their productivity. They become vulnerable to burnout. Be sure to maintain an open dialogue about the level of engagement and challenge the older worker has with his work. A younger worker will tell you he is bored in a New York minute. Not so a Boomer.

Feedback for the Boss

Most younger managers desire feedback on their own performance from their employees. Actually, all good managers should strive to elicit feedback, but younger managers are just more direct and energetic about asking for it. Communicating upward to one's boss is always difficult, but it is especially hard for a Boomer to engage in this type of dialogue with a younger manager. John Eldrege in *Wild at Heart* talks about being given a chance to provide his boss some feedback long after he had left a position and could do it without worrying about negative consequences:

> *I had a chance a few years back to tell my boss what I really thought of him, not in sinful anger (there is a difference), not to hurt him but to help him. He actually asked me to, called to see if I was free to chat for a moment. I knew what he was calling for and I ran, I told him I was busy.*

Most Boomers would avoid a conversation like that one; however, the real problem is that older workers are not communicating less threatening information upward. They do not initiate conversations with younger managers at times for fear of seeming to be telling the manager what to do or of being guilty of TMI (Too Much Information).

Be sure you are encouraging upward communication from your older workers. In most cases, you will need to be the initiator and coach in this communication process.

The Top 10 Motivators for Boomers vs. Gen X

Boomers	Generation X
1. Good wages	1. Appreciation
2. Job security	2. Feeling in on things
3. Promotion opportunities	3. Understanding attitude
4. Good working conditions	4. Job security
5. Interesting work	5. Good wages
6. Loyalty from management	6. Interesting work
7. Tactful discipline	7. Promotion opportunities
8. Appreciation	8. Loyalty from management
9. Understanding attitude	9. Good working conditions
10. Feeling in on things	10. Tactful discipline

—From "Leading Answers," by Robin Robertson

Assessing the Success of Motivation

Motivational strategies are worthless if you do not asssess if they work. Motivational moves you make are not just to increase performance for the company but for the success and satisfaction of the employee himself; therefore, don't make the assessment threatening. During my first job as a management consultant with a large firm, one of my cohorts was fired forthwith for walking around with a clipboard making notes on every employee's productivity. Now that is threatening.

Still, both you and the employee should agree on some ways of measuring what needs to be improved. If you try some motivational strategies yet performance does not improve, you simply may need to meet with the employee and find other ways to advance strong performance. Try to tie the performance improvement to numbers: number of documents processed, dollar increase in sales volume, or percentage decrease in customer service complaints.

Motivation, whether successful or not, should be revisited at least a couple of times a year. Even the best employees need to be motivated.

Great Employees Need Motivation

The best employees usually receive the least motivation. Because there are no immediate problems with good employees, they do not receive the attention or motivating rewards most weaker performers receive. The consequences of failing to motivate great employees are costly:

- They may lose their incentive to perform well.
- They may leave to work for someone who will focus on them more.
- They may adjust their level of performance to that of the weaker employees.

Whatever the age or performance level of the employee, your job as manager will always be to motivate. Just because an older worker does not badger you for more challenging work or better rewards, don't think his performance can be sustained without motivation. Engage him in a conversation about what motivation means to him as a starting point.

Management Communication Opportunities

Some communication opportunities are more defined. Communication opportunities like staff meetings and performance appraisals are more like events, and carry with them some strong expectations from your employees. Older employees especially have predefined expectations for the feedback they expect from you as a manager and for the way you will develop them while they report to you. Preparing for these events and processes is critical if you are to lead a team effectively. You can leverage these opportunities to gain an older employee's respect and to further enhance the communication between you if you approach each strategically.

Opportunity 1: Generational Differences in Meetings

In their heads, Boomers have a vision of what a meeting should look like based on tradition, etiquette, and, in part, some very good business reasons. You have a totally different model based on speed, efficiency, and a semi-synchronous communication model. Here is how the models differ:

Boomer Meeting Model
- A set agenda should be followed strictly.
- Every meeting should have a leader. Meeting speakers should have a presentation and should meet expected time limits.
- No one except the person taking minutes should be typing while the speaker is speaking. An open laptop or a PDA in front of an attendee is proof that you are not paying attention and is an affront.
- You should maintain uninterrupted eye contact with the leader of the meeting.
- Seniority and level in the company dictate who is listened to and not interrupted.

- The best meetings feature great speakers/leaders who address an audience of attendees. The tone is extremely businesslike.

Gen-XY Meeting Model
- Collaborative meetings are best. Being flexible to follow new and creative ideas will lead to innovation.
- A meeting really doesn't need a leader or speaker. Loosely structured meetings can allow various team members just to show up and share. If you show up and there really isn't much to talk about, it is fine to adjourn in five minutes. If the team, however, is communicating freely, then the leaders should not try to authoritatively enforce time limits. This is anti-team and anti-communication.
- Having your laptop/PDA in front of you is the best way to take notes and retain information. And what is the big deal if someone IMs you during the meeting and you shoot a two-word answer?
- Eye contact is not given consistently or at all because you may be typing or you may be connecting with a friend in the meeting.
- Interruptions are good if they result in a more efficient use of your time. You may have something valuable to consider that could change the direction of the entire meeting. Weak premises should be addressed as soon as possible to achieve the most efficient meeting possible.
- The best meetings are interactive and kind of fun.

Creating Great Meetings for All Generations
Somewhere between the two models above is the perfect meeting. Each generation thinks its way is far more efficient and productive than the other. For instance, younger workers are absolutely correct that people retain more information when the meeting is interactive, collaborative, flexible, and kind

of fun. On the other hand, in the debriefing that my Gen-XY students turn in after their team presentations in my business communication class at Georgia State, there is only one thing that almost all say they would do differently next time: They would have an agenda for each meeting.

So how do you incorporate the best of both models? The blend of the following two models will lead to collaborative yet structured meetings that should leverage the efficiencies both generations value.

Multigenerational Meeting Model

1. **Create an agenda but entitle it Proposed Agenda.** Demonstrate that you have a plan; that will gain the respect of the Boomers and inspire their confidence that the meeting will be productive. Still, the word *proposed* holds out hope to younger workers that room will be made for their spontaneous and creative ideas. That one word sends a message that they can help shape the meeting and that you will still work flexibly with them, even though you have a black-and-white agenda the older crowd finds more professional.

2. **Prior to the meeting, circulate the agenda via e-mail.** Ask for additions and ideas. Start the collaboration early.

3. **At the meeting, distribute the revised Proposed Agenda.** State that the topics listed are your understanding of what needs to be addressed in this meeting but ask for any new ideas or collaboration that anyone feels cannot wait until the next meeting. Express the desire to be flexible but to have a working plan as a general guide to keep the meeting on track.

4. **Express respect and value for the input and ideas of each person** and ask for everyone's attention for the time period of the meeting.

5. **Ask that all cell phones and PDAs be turned off during meetings.** If this is a problem to do for an hour, perhaps you need to shorten your meeting. Or, ask younger workers to put an automatic reply on their e-mail/IM to tell contacts to call your administrative assistant if there is an emergency. Employees in sales in particular do not want to be inaccessible to their customers. Offering the services of a live human being to deal with these messages may be a good solution.

6. **Are you sure you are having someone take excellent minutes?** Perhaps if you are, the other attendees will not feel the need to type during the meeting.

7. **Start on time but start with a noncritical item.** You do not want to miss the valuable input of employees who may not be punctual. Yet, if you do not start when you said you would, many Boomers will feel their time is not being respected and you will also be reinforcing the lack of punctuality. Tardy employees are often innovative and valuable employees; time management is their issue and you don't want to forego their contributions to critical topics.

8. **Although the first agenda item should be a noncritical topic, all topics that must be resolved should be listed early on the agenda.** If the meeting begins to go long, you should attempt to give any employee the option to leave if he has another meeting scheduled. If you have planned the agenda correctly, all important items will have been addressed. The full staff does not need to be in attendance for less-important topics. And besides, if you have assigned a proficient taker of minutes, the departing employees can find the information in the minutes.

9. **Build in interactivity.** Do not speak for more than 25 percent of the meeting. Ask other teammates to address items so that you don't have to speak. Create activities and games to share information. Online bookstores can

give you many ideas for training games, ice breakers, and other interactive meeting ideas.

10. **Use an interactive technique to brainstorm so that every employee, even the quietest one, has input.** The nominal group technique is an excellent way to arrive at group consensus and there are many versions of this approach online. The Boomer's love the structure and the younger employees love the collaborative and inclusive nature of it.

11. **End with next steps or action items.** Send these to everyone within twenty-four hours of the meeting.

Finding the right balance of structure and free-form collaboration and fun is an art and not a science. With each team you manage, you will have to discover what works for that unique group. Use the previous model as a starting point and then listen and observe. Your instincts and the input from your team will help you design meetings that will work well for multigenerational teams.

But then again, why even have meetings? Your generation is much more likely to find an alternative to the traditional business meeting in any number of creative ways: videoconferencing, webcasts, and blogs are just a few meeting alternatives.

Meeting and Communicating in Your Own Style

Don't you think most meetings are a waste of time? Of course you do. While all generations feel this way, yours is the generation that has the tools to do something about it. And meetings are not the only communication vehicle changing. Because the generations differ on what good communication is (largely based on their differences regarding what being relational is) we are in a vortex of change in business communication of all kinds. Be creative about experimenting with ways to conduct meetings using technology. The key to blending in some of these new ways of meeting, like webcasts, videoconferences, and conference calls, is in taking the time to prepare the older worker to be a successful participant in the meeting. That may require some training or some coaching from you, but the time spent could be a good way to build the trust and communication between you.

Opportunity 2: *Career Counseling, Professional Development, and Performance Appraisals*

One of your responsibilities to your staff is to develop them professionally. Development is divided into two categories:

Category 1: Development that results in improving the employee's salary, level in the company (promotions), breadth of responsibility, or title.

Category 2: Development of professional and personal skills or abilities that make the employee more valuable, more successful in his relationships and responsiblities, and that can perhaps prepare him for future movement either laterally or upward in the organization.

Some of the best management you will ever do will be in development sessions. In these sessions, you have the opportunity to demonstrate your sincere interest in the employee's success and contentment within your company and department. You can prove your belief in her by investing this time and perhaps other resources, thus showing her that she is valued.

But development is not easy. First, you have to communicate honestly and sensitively with the employee regarding his areas of strengths and weaknesses. It is critical to reinforce strengths. If you do not continue to build on existing strengths, in most cases those strengths will diminish. But addressing strengths is the easy part.

Developing areas of weakness is more challenging. To pin-point which areas to address in a development session, look at all of your sources of information:

- 360-degree surveys
- Past performance appraisals
- Challenges with people and projects over the last year
- Assessments and testing
- Observations and conversations

The most important source of input, however, is the employee himself. Older workers are usually extremely honest about their developmental needs. Every developmental session should begin with asking the employee what he would like to improve. A typical agenda follows:

Agenda for a Developmental Session
1. **Warmly greet the employee.**
2. **Acknowledge accomplishments and strengths demonstrated in the past year.** State that you want to support the employee in continuing to build on those strengths. For example, if the employee is strong in networking with other departments, tell him you want him to serve on an interdepartmental task force that is forming so that he can continue to build strong relationships for your department.
3. **At first, talk briefly to the employee about his career, not his job.** Be sure to clarify that you are not encouraging him to move on or he might feel you have a hidden agenda. Just express that you have been trained to periodically review your own career and you want to help him look at what his future might hold. Boomer employees were not trained to speak up for themselves or to look intentionally for the next career move. This may be stressful for an older employee to discuss, so be sure you reassure him

that you are only sharing the expertise you use when managing your own career. Offer to get the employee training or interdepartmental exposure that might help him with a future career move. Discuss the value of lateral moves that can make him more agile and valuable in the internal job market. This concept of lateral moves for development may be something the Boomer has not previously considered.

For employees who have never had a manager express interest in their careers, this conversation centered on their career path can be an extremely valuable one. For those who desire to be mentored or developed, your interest will be deeply appreciated. I can think of no more gratifying conversation that can increase the respect an older worker has for a younger manager. Naturally, communication flows much more freely and positively when the employee realizes you are interested in her for more than the set of tasks she does each day.

1. **Ask the employee what she has identified as her developmental needs.** Give her time to discuss these her way and in her own time. This is not a discussion that should be rushed.
2. **Then ask her what she thinks would be helpful to strengthen these areas.**
3. **When the employee has fully expressed herself, offer your observations if necessary.** I say "if necessary" because many managers find that the employee has already brought up everything important regarding developmental needs. And often, the employee has even better ideas than you do for training she can take or other developmental steps to correct any problems. If she has covered most of the feedback you had planned to give her, then hold back on saying much. Just agree with her that these are good ideas to strengthen her developmental areas. She will have

much stronger commitment to working on improving if the developmental steps she is taking were her idea and not yours.

4. **If the employee has not addressed a developmental area then you must.** Explain that the area you want her to improve will help make her more valuable to the department as well as in her own career. Put the need in the context that everyone has developmental needs and that this discussion should be viewed as a positive investment in her future. Describe the need without comparison to specific individuals in the department and without judgmental or personal criticisms. Be very objective, citing instances and facts. Then suggest developmental coaching, training, job shadowing, or other avenues to help the employee develop excellence in this area. Coaching can be by peers, experts, or yourself. Other developmental resources include audio programs, online learning, seminars, and books.

5. **At the end of the session, state any firm expectations you have of the employee.** Set time limits for getting some things accomplished. Agree to get back together in a month or three months to evaluate progress.

6. **End by very specifically affirming the expertise and traits that make this employee valuable.** Cite examples from the past year that demonstrated her worth and abilities. It is important to keep a file of these incidences for each employee because we do tend to forget. Thank the employee for her contributions.

The previous session can be altered to include a performance appraisal. You follow the same agenda except for the appraisal itself. After Step 3 or 4, present the blank appraisal tool you use. Often, the tool will have number ratings. On the blank appraisal, ask the employee to rate himself. Compare what he listed with what you marked. Discuss the differences. Again,

many Boomers rank themselves lower than their managers rank them. If the Boomer has ranked himself higher on an item, discuss what led both of you to your rating. Be open to changing the rating if the employee makes a good point.

Set some expectations for improvement in very concrete terms. For example, specify the number of errors that should be reduced or the percentage of improvement in quality you require. End with your expression of confidence in the employee. Resume the rest of the development session as stated. If you think that the employee will be very upset by his performance appraisal, consider handling the session differently:

- Conduct the performance appraisal at a separate meeting.
- Conduct the performance appraisal at the end of the meeting. He may not hear all of the developmental information if he becomes upset early in the session.

Opportunity 3: Feedback

A great deal of feedback will take place in the development session, but you should not wait for this session to offer developmental feedback. Feedback, consisting of compliments, how-tos, and constructive criticism, should be an ongoing dialogue between you and your employee. One of the basic rights and needs of an employee is to know how she is doing. Sadly, many employees work with nagging worries and insecurities because the manager fails to tell them they are doing a good job. You would think they would know, but until the manager validates what they are doing, many employees are adrift in self-doubt.

The first rule of feedback is that it should be timely—immediate if possible. Feedback on a job well done or behaviors that need to be improved should be woven into the fabric of every workday. An employee should not have to wait for weeks not knowing that you are really dissatisfied with the way he is organizing something. In addition, holding back feedback will frustrate you and hurt your performance. When enployees realize that you are going to give them feedback frequently, they usually become more comfortable with it. On-the-go feedback is much less stressful than being called into the office for a rare but unpleasant talk about one's performance.

Communicate constantly about individual and team performance. Talk about teamwork and goals. These sessions are also good for discussing TWWDTN (The Way We Do Things Now). Boomers may have had to change from systems and practices they really think were better. Feedback sessions are a good way to dicuss positives about the new ways of doing things and to elicit the Boomer's suggestions on how to work out the kinks of anything new.

Boomers and Feedback

Boomers are less comfortable with feedback than previous generations. Don't expect these feedback sessions to be comfortable or welcome at first. Unlike in your generation, the school systems did not stress giving ongoing constructive feedback when the Boomers were in school. And in the early years of a Boomer's career, the only feedback was probably negative, so for them, there is usually a feeling of dread associated with the word feedback.

Also, most Boomers feel a bit awkward with compliments and positive feedback. Does that surprise you? Everyone from parents to teachers to coaches were taught to give positive feedback to your generation; not so for Boomers. Don't let their awkard or even uncomfortable response to your positive feedback discourage dialogue. They will eventually get used to it. And though they might doubt your sincerity at first, your continued interest and investment in their performance will eventually win them over.

Opportunity 4: Problem-Solving and Decision-Making

Whereas your generation has a higher expectation of being part of the decision-making process, you may need to draw Boomers into it. It's not that they don't want their input considered; they just don't feel right asking to be heard. They may be passive out of respect for you and never express something they feel strongly about.

The older worker's view of the work world is very much one of top-down communication. In their view, you as a manager will tell them what to do. And if you want an answer to a question, they figure you will ask them. And even if you tell them that the communication should be flowing up, down, and sideways, you will probably have to train them to brainstorm and collaborate. Still, drawing them into the decision-making process will make them much more committed to any decisions made. Don't let their reticence stop you. Some suggestions for bringing the Boomer employee into the process follow.

Brainstorming

Consider having group brainstorming sessions periodically. Here are the rules:

1. **You throw out a problem and ask for solutions.** Someone, maybe you, takes down all the ideas on a flip chart or dry erase board that is large so everyone can see. You can't do this exercise on your laptop.
2. **Every idea, no matter how unrealistic, goes on the page.** You can't discuss in detail the ideas until a complete list is gathered. Encourage broad participation. Don't let one or two people monopolize. Ask individuals who are not participating, "What do you think?"
3. **Only after all ideas are listed should you begin to be critical.** There are many ways to begin to pare down the list. You can divide the items on the list according to who owns

them. Mark the ones that you must do with "M" for manager. Divvy up the rest according to departments or responsibilities. Or, you can eliminate the ones that are impossible, but be very careful before you do that. Some of the most performance-enhancing ideas in business start with ideas that look impossible initially.

4. **Consider using the nominal group technique (NGT) mentioned earlier that ensures that everyone's ideas are considered.** If you do not know how to implement NGT, this technique has been widely written about in college textbooks and online.

5. **Gradually hone in on one or two good ideas.** You may want to assign team members to research the ideas and schedule another session for the team to decide what to do.

This type of brainstorming session is just one of many ways to include older workers in the decision-making process. Evaluating the risks and rewards through a matrix and discussing the potential for both is another way to evaluate ideas.

Informal Problem-Solving

Informal inclusion can be just as powerful as formal problem-solving techniques. Call a Boomer into your office and tell her about a decision you must make. Tell her your options and ask for advice. Even if the employee does not solve your problem, the respect you have shown her will improve your mutual communication.

Coordinating Versus Planning

Because today's younger managers are living in a faster-paced world where multitasking is common and change is even more inevitable, your role requires more coordinating of people and resources than planning. In previous decades, plans could be made further in advance and would usually be executed pretty much as designed. Not so today. Your job as a manager today is more to coordinate the resources you have and to deploy them in the most effective way possible given the circumstances. Being flexible and creative in the use of your resources is more important today than the ability to create detailed project plans.

Interestingly, the Boomers have succeeded in creating participatory households that include their Generation Y offspring in family decision-making from an early age. These Yers arrive in the workplace prepared to contribute and collaborate. Managers with a "my way or the highway" style risk losing these younger workers and their potential contributions to their organizations.

—*Lee Ann H. Webster, "Sharpen Your Communication Skills"*

Thoughts on Different Approaches and Motivations

The following are actual comments related to directing the work of older employees and motivating them. All comments were written in by respondents to the XYBoom Survey. Only a representative sample of answers is included.

- You need to demonstrate that you are a leader without being a boss.
- Sometimes they need to be specifically told to do something—union worker mentality. In that case, I spell things out specifically, offer recognition for achievement, and find more for them to do ASAP.

- Older workers expect to be treated with respect and courtesy. Many do not like to be "bossed"; they want to be made to feel like they have added value, more so than younger workers. Younger workers want to be given more direction and a better understanding of their goals; they want very clear and concise directions so that there is no question as to the outcome. But in the end you need to manage personality more so than age. Everyone is different: different motivations, backgrounds, education, experience, and learning ability.

- It just seems like things really need to be laid out for them instead of being self-explanatory.

- I have had good and bad experiences. I managed one lady who wouldn't do anything without getting permission. She was supposed to be overseeing her department, but she would come to me for every decision. I finally had to remove her from that position because she wouldn't make any relevant decisions. I guess I would suggest that you take a chance. Sometimes it is better to ask forgiveness than permission. Just do what you think is best, stand up for what you believe, and keep an open mind.

- You need to be forward with older workers. They can be set in their ways but usually have some valuable insights and contributions.

- Older workers are less likely to adhere to "political correctness" and instead speak their mind with less concern about how their opinions may be interpreted. That can occasionally be problematic for obvious reasons.

- Developing clear work plans has assisted in alleviating this issue.

- The biggest issue I have faced is making sure my assistant shares her thoughts and is not afraid of speaking in team meetings. To help with this I have made each staff member be in charge of a portion of the meeting. This empowers the staff.

Dos and Don'ts

Do be open, interested in the person regardless of age, solicitous of input, and open to his ideas. Simultaneously, be the leader you were hired to be—give direction but don't be bossy in your style.

Do develop definitive work plans for all your employees but especially for older workers.

Do be very direct in giving work objectives but maintain courtesy and respect. In the continuum between asking and telling employees what to do, younger workers tend to want to be asked and older workers may tend to wait to be told. There is no stereotype, so learn about your employee before leaning to either extreme on the ask-tell continuum.

Do be explicit in explaining to your older workers that you want them to show more initiative in moving forward and foregoing permission on minor steps.

Do read Chapter 6 for strategies for giving direction to older workers.

Don't punish or enforce consequences when your older workers are first experimenting with taking risks and showing greater initiative. You can tell them what they should have done as you commend them for taking the risk, even when they misstep. That is why it is a risk.

CHAPTER 7

Trust, Respect, Etiquette, and Office Politics

Nothing can make people ruder than when they believe you have been rude to them. Respect. Courtesy. Workplace etiquette. Whatever you want to call it, every generation desires thoughtful treatment and regard for their feelings, time, and worth. It's just that each generation comes at this much-misunderstood subject from extremely different perspectives. Different viewpoints lead to a great deal of "you're wrong, I'm right" thinking on the part of all ages. The following are fifteen ways you differ from your older employees in the areas of etiquette and office politics. Before you dismiss these concepts as unimportant or superficial, stop and consider this: Trust and respect for this generation are demonstrated in the following fifteen ways. Likewise, if you make no attempt to meet the Boomers halfway on some of these issues, their respect for you will be similarly damaged. Trying to develop some of the habits that Boomers value so highly might be worth the investment.

Way 1: Respect for the Boss and Peers

Your generation believes that respect is earned through performance and not longevity. You will admire and appreciate the accomplishments of anyone, no matter if he is new on the job and barely eighteen years old.

Boomers will appreciate the younger workers as well, but they believe older workers have a special thing going for them: seniority. In the Boomer mind, just being a senior employee entitles a person to some respect. It makes sense to them that if a person has been around a long time, he has accumulated wisdom and expertise. This virtual vault of treasures can be called upon as needed in all kinds of situations, and they expect younger employees to regard them with appreciation just for being there and being rich with experience.

The following generational assessment of whether or not the boss is always right comes from John Bishop's "Are Your Managers Ready for Generation Y?":

Boomers: The boss is not always right, but the boss is always the boss. I will put in long hours to get ahead. If necessary, I will do so at the expense of my family.

Generation X: The boss is not always right, but I'm not going to be here very long. I watched my parents' jobs be downsized or outsourced so I don't have the same loyalty to a company they did. I'm not married to the company; I value my life outside of work.

Generation Y: The boss is not always right, but is she open to new ways to do business? Events like 9/11 and the Columbine High School shooting have taught us that life can be fleeting. The Internet has exposed us to new ways of approaching life and work.

Though Boomers have shown an amazing receptivity to be managed by younger managers, older workers don't always realize that younger employees are rich with experience as well, despite their fewer years in the workplace. Younger employees have been gaining valuable experience related to diversity, technology, and teamwork from the time they were in preschool. Young and old have experience to offer, so Gen-XYers don't see the need to treat Boomers as if their experience is more valuable. Gen-XYers want to treat Boomers as colleagues and equals.

To some Boomers, this lack of regard for their age and experience feels like a direct insult. They don't see this as a different perspective but as an intentional slight. This problem is being exacerbated as young managers are being given preferential treatment due to the war for talent. Corporations are so panicked by the statistical projections that tell them there are too few Gen-XY managers who can replace the Boomers who are retiring that they are incenting younger workers in any way possible. Business just does not have the same motivation to promote older workers.

Way 2: Your Direct Questions Can Seem Like a Challenge

For many years, I have taught in professional development leadership programs aimed at young professionals. Some of my *Fortune* 500 clients hire young professionals, usually straight from MBA programs. For two decades, I was introduced at my seminars by the program directors who would give my short biography and perhaps tell the group that I had been a trusted consultant of the company for ten to twenty years. About four years ago, this intro stopped working well. I remember teaching a group about business communication when shortly after the session started a twenty-something man abruptly said,

"Who are you?" In years past, it had been enough that I was trusted by the older and established management of their program and by the executives of their company. This young man really wanted to know for himself what my credentials were. What was relevant to him about my experience? Why should he spend time listening to me?

Fortunately, I recognized his abrupt question as just that—a real question with a desire for a real answer. I told him about a few of my projects that would be similar to projects he had been assigned to for the next four months. I kept each example short. I ended each example with evidence of tangible results: profits, customer feedback, new business won, and lots of numbers attesting to my effectiveness. The concrete examples, tailored to his level, job assignment, and interests, brought instant support from this young man and influenced the rest of the class very positively.

More than 60% of employers say they are experiencing tension between employees from different generations, according to a survey by Lee Hecht Harrison. The survey found more than 70% of older employees are dismissive of younger workers' abilities. And nearly half of employers say that younger employees are dismissive of the abilities of their older co-workers.

—Stephanie Armour,
"Generation Y: They've Arrived at Work with a New Attitude"

What a Question Is and Isn't
Where many Boomers make their mistake is in not recognizing a question as just a question. Your questions are not

attempts to find flaws in the Boomer's information, but it may feel that way to the Boomer. Your questions are not a challenge to her authority. You really aren't concerned with authority; rather, your focus is on getting the best decisions made for greater productivity. Still, the Gen-XY machine gun style of asking lots of questions can feel like a direct attack on a Boomer's credibility. How do you fix this and still find out the answers to your questions?

A Questioning Style that Works for Boomers

1. **Begin by stating that you find the information valuable and interesting.** Tell the Boomer it is so interesting that you would like to know more.

2. **Ask if he minds if you ask some questions to help you really grasp what he is saying.** Tell him that your style of collaboration sometimes involves pinging. Pinging is taking one person's idea, playing with it, asking questions about it (including "what if" questions), and bouncing (pinging) more ideas off the person you are talking to.

3. **Invite him to ask you questions as the process of pinging goes on during your conversation.**

4. **Try to preface your questions with a few words to soften the thrust of the question:** "I see," "That makes sense," "That is great/interesting/so valid," "I never thought of it in that way," or "You have hit on something there."

5. **If possible, try to give the questions a rest from time to time and just have some content laden conversation that involves no questions.** Boomers need a break from so much inquisition.

6. **At the end, tell the Boomer again that you hope he understands that the barrage of questions you ask is just your learning style.** Thank him for being patient and for teaching you a great deal about the particular project.

What your generation considers an asset can actually be considered a communication liability to some Boomers. So many questions may feel like high-energy brainstorming to you, but it can feel threatening to an older worker.

Your way of showing you are engaged and genuinely interested in a project may be to ask lots of questions. To the older worker, you may seem to be picking his ideas and actions apart, and the questions can feel very critical. Your intent may be just the opposite, but perceptions and feelings on this subject run strong.

Don't stop asking those good questions. Questions can take a good idea and make it great or anticipate obstacles and ensure success. Just adapt your style as suggested earlier.

Way 3: Your Suggestions Can Sound Like Micromanagement

Another by-product of your education in the era of brainstorming and collaboration is that you think people of all ages will value your suggestions. Quite often they do not. Boomers particularly may feel you are demeaning them or second-guessing their solutions if you are not careful about the way you make suggestions. Be sure you demonstrate that you value what the Boomer says before making any suggestions. Try to form the suggestion as a question: "In your twenty years of experience here at Acme, has anyone ever tried it this alternative way?"

Way 4: Careful! Your Self-Esteem Is Showing

Gen-XY managers also have another perception to fight that is common among Boomer employees. Your generations were brought up to have high self-esteem. Boomers were brought up to demonstrate humility, whether it was genuine or not. Their parents were fond of sayings like "You are no better than anyone else," "Don't get too big for your britches," and "The bigger they are, the harder they fall." Contrast that to all the school and family programs aimed at teaching you to value yourself, to believe in yourself, and to know that you had unique and special gifts that no one else could contribute quite like you. You can see how the generations would have philosophical clashes.

When you talk about your skills and abilities, be sure to mention first that everyone on the team brings unique gifts prior to talking about yours. Your job is to raise the self-esteem of your employees, so invest much more time in that than in describing your own assets. On team projects in college, you were taught to assess your strengths quickly and offer them to the team. Boomers were taught never to mention their gifts. They had to wait until someone else discovered their gifts and then hope that person would mention their assets. It was against "the Rules" to mention your own talents, giving rise to some of the most circuitous game-playing in workplace history. Summarizing one's own talents and expertise and offering that wealth to the team was considered bragging. With that in mind, be careful about the initial conversations you have with older employees about what you have to offer.

Way 5: Entitlement

Closely related to self-esteem issues is the perception Boomers have that Gen-XY managers come to work with a sense of entitlement. One reason this feeling arises is that younger managers quite often enter the job market with skills developed for the workplace of today—skills in technology, various languages, and other expertise with a marketable value. As mentioned previously, when your generation entered the workplace with these assets, the Boomers saw you and your peers placed in positions that they had to work years to earn through the old seniority system. Today's workplace does not work on the seniority system, for the most part, and intellectually the Boomer understands this. Still, the Boomers paid their dues under the old seniority system, and just when their payoff should have arrived, the system was changed to a more performance-based one. Although the Boomer will not blame you, there are some residual bad feelings from this loss many have experienced due to the marketplace not keeping its end of the bargain. All may lie dormant until you feel you should be promoted even faster. One comment like, "I have been a supervisor for three years and should be a manager by now" may be fighting words if the Boomer had to wait ten years for a similar promotion or if you got the supervisor's position he would have been grateful for.

Matt Berkley, 24, a writer at St. Louis Small Business Monthly, says many of his generation have traveled and had many enriching experiences, so they may clash with older generations they see as competition or not as skilled. . . . "It seems like our parents just groomed us. . . . But they deprived us of social skills. They don't treat older employees as well as they should."

—Stephanie Armour,

"Generation Y: They've Arrived at Work with a New Attitude"

Being sensitive to this feeling is about all you can do. If you need to cry on someone's shoulder about your career advancement not being all you hoped for, find someone your own age to complain to. A Boomer is not the best choice for this conversation.

Coaching Older Employees to Package Themselves Better

Using caution in mentioning your gifts and expertise does not mean that you should not offer that information at all. Not only should you communicate what you have to offer, but you should also be teaching older employees to do the same. Older employees can learn from you the ways to let the rest of the organization know about the expertise and information they can contribute. It is especially important that older employees learn this self-marketing today. With mergers and downsizing, no one should be keeping his marketable assets a secret.

Show the older employee how to package herself as a valuable asset by doing the following:

1. Take older employees to interdepartmental meetings to offer brief information from their areas of expertise.
2. Make sure all employees have an up-to-date resume with a section at the top that highlights special skills and abilities. Be careful how you bring this up, however, or employees will think they are about to be fired.
3. Do a survey that invites 360-degree feedback about what each employee is valued for by bosses, peers, and others.
4. See if your HR department has other tools that will help the older employee identify marketable skills and abilities.
5. Ask employees to list the three projects that they are proudest of; then go back and help them list all the abilities they demonstrated to make each project a success: project management, motivations, influence, desktop publishing, marketing, strategic planning, and facilitation, to name just a few.

Way 6: Work-Life Balance

Work-life balance isn't just a buzzword. Unlike Boomers who tend to put a high priority on career, today's youngest workers are more interested in making their jobs accommodate their family and personal lives. They want jobs with flexibility, tele-commuting options, and the ability to go part-time or leave the work force temporarily when children are in the picture.

"There's a higher value on self-fulfillment," says Diana San Diego, twenty-four, who lives with her parents in San Francisco and works on college campuses helping prepare students for the working world through the Parachute College Program. "After 9/11, there is a realization that life is short. You value it more."

—Stephanie Armour,
"Generation Y: They've Arrived at Work with a New Attitude"

Make sure that balance is achieved by all age groups you manage. Problems grow when managers achieve that balance while older workers are putting in long hours.

Way 7: Communicating to Higher Levels

You know that great ideas can come from people at any level. That is why younger employees are not timid when commu-nicating with executives and others several levels above their pay grade. After all, younger generations were told by their parents that their ideas were creative and bright. Older genera-tions were brought up in a family hierarchy that stressed the idea that "children are to be seen and not heard."

In many ways, our hierarchy at work tends to emulate the hierarchy of our families. That is just one of the reasons Boomers feel that the CEO is probably not interested in what they have to say. More important to you as a manager, the Boomer may feel that she is waiting for you to invite her ideas. For Boomers, waiting to be asked for information is more of a matter of respecting your position (an outdated concept) than of lacking initiative.

Bruce Tulgan, who coauthored *Managing Generation Y* with Carolyn Martin and leads training sessions at companies on how to prepare for and retain Gen-Yers, says a recent example is a young woman who just started a job at a cereal company. She showed up the first day with a recipe for a new cereal she'd invented.

Way 8: Multitasking

Another differing view of office etiquette that can be attributed to familial teaching is the perspectives on multitasking. Your generation sees multitasking as a virtue, a skill, and a vital ability if you are to get all your work completed, goals met, and still have some work-life balance.

Boomers see multitasking that takes your undivided attention away from a conversation or an important task as counterproductive. When you are simultaneously texting and talking and keeping your eye on the Dow Jones tape running across your laptop screen, the Boomer doubts you can be effective. See Chapter 6 to understand how to form the relationship with your older employees that will make them trust you to do some of these activities simultaneously. And you might just consider that they do have a point at times. Re-examine to assess whether the task or person really does deserve or require your undivided attention.

Way 9: Earphones, Cell Phones, iPods, and Other Reasons You Are Not Listening

One sight that most Boomers feel is highly unprofessional is you with an earbud or Bluetooth device stuck in your ear. First, he doesn't feel that you should be listening to music at work at all. Secondly, if you must listen, you can't possibly be thinking straight with that loud, distracting noise in your ear. Earphones of any type give the false impression that you are not working but goofing off.

It is disconcerting for an older employee when you are in his presence with a Bluetooth device in your ear. His thoughts are: "Is she connected to someone right now? Does she have to bring her personal life into the workplace so pervasively that she keeps her receiver in her ear?" and "Is she doing that to look cool?"

At the bottom of this conflict between older workers and their younger managers is the older worker's fear of being disregarded and made to feel inconsequential. Your intent may be just to listen to music, but the message, erroneous or not, you send to the employee is that his input is so lightweight that you can absorb it with half a brain. This feeling may not be accurate, but it is a widely held feeling among older workers.

In the privacy of your office, go for it, but when you are engaged with older employees, leave the earphones behind.

As you get to know the employee better, you can say something like, "When I am working on my expense reports, I always listen to music. For some reason, I work faster with music." You don't owe the older worker an explanation, but communicating about your work habits might lead to his understanding you better. Understanding always leads to better communication, so what's to lose?

Way 10: Work Ethic and Long-Term Job Commitment

Generations X, Y, and Boomer all have strong work ethics, but their work style is all over the map with differences. The younger generations tend to feel that work does not need to be done from 8:30 until 5:30, while most of the older generation still feels that the traditional workday has its merits. They eye each other with wariness regarding who is actually getting the most work done. Interestingly enough, however, once alternative schedules and telecommuting are introduced into the workplace, older workers participate fully. See Chapter 3 for more on the issue of time and timing.

Way 11: Cynicism

Similarly, your realistic and blunt assessment of situations and your direct conversational style may cause the Boomer to think you are cynical or negative. You are not pessimistic; you are just aware that change happens and that your job, as you now know it, may not exist tomorrow. Your generation was molded by bombings by terrorists and even from factions within our own citizenry as in the Oklahoma bombings. The Virginia Tech massacre is just one of many incidents of school violence. A person's world can change in a day, and living for today makes more sense.

Just because you know that the political and financial balance can shift quickly doesn't mean you are pessimistic, but you can sound that way to older employees. When you are being brutally honest about potential problems and insecurities in the department, be sure to be careful how you phrase it. Let the older employee know when you are talking about worst-case scenarios that you do not expect these to actually happen. Always offer a positive outcome as a possibility as well. You are more confident about your ability to roll with anything that occurs. Conversations about possible events that could mean a job loss or change will probably result in many sleepless nights for a Boomer. Is that really the way to get top performance from the older worker?

Way 12: Humor Differences

Closely related to cynicism is the huge difference in what many Boomers find funny and what many younger managers consider funny. Generations X and Y tend to have an edge to their humor that can seem a bit harsh or even inappropriate to older employees. Because content of media was mostly G-rated when the Boomers were growing up, they may be shocked by cartoons, websites, jokes, or pictures that you find appropriate for the workplace.

The comics of Generations X and Y and other trendsetters have even changed the vocabulary of what is good and bad. If your generation says something is sick, ridiculous, or insane, that is a good thing. The Boomer tends to think these are not conditions to strive for.

Another thing that comedians and others have made acceptable to younger generations is to joke about flaws or habits that make a person unique. This razzing may not be funny to an older employee, and it could even lead to an embarrassing situation or even legal action if taken out of context.

There are many things both you and your older employee can find humorous. Stick to those and avoid any that might make the employee uncomfortable. If you think you may have crossed the line, open up a conversation with the employee. Say, "When I was teasing you about buying that hot tub the other day, I think I made you uncomfortable. I'd like to apologize." The employee can confirm his discomfort or let you know he is not uncomfortable. Err on the side of caution.

Way 13: Profanity

Because you have been inundated with profanity in everything from kid's movies like *Home Alone* to blogs and websites, you may not be overly sensitive to profanity. Your Boomer employee is. Avoid profanity in the workplace. This is one area where your Boomer has the right idea.

Way 14: Dress Codes

If you have ever worn flip-flops, a tight T-shirt, jeans, or Capri pants to the office, you may have already made your older employees doubt your good judgment. And if you have bared anything from shoulders to midriff you may have set off alarm bells in their minds regarding your ethics and morals. This antiquated thinking may be funny to you, but as a leader you want your people to trust your judgment. Keep in mind that your dress did not matter as much when you were an individual contributor. As a supervisor or manager, your professional image is important. Be sure you wear those Capri pants only to annual picnics and cover up bare midriffs and backs.

After all, younger managers have some admitted challenges gaining respect from older workers. Do you really want the battle to be about how low you wear your pants? Don't you want your exchanges with older workers to be more substantive than that?

You may be right about your fashion sense for today's times, but you will not stop an older worker from having doubts about your wisdom. Keep the focus on the work issues and what you have to offer as a professional by avoiding petty differences about dress. Keep the main thing the main thing. This is one you can't fight. Those mental images are just there in a Boomer's mind and will stay there until you refuse to make your dress an issue. You can avoid this entire problem by dressing more conservatively.

Way 15: Money Issues

Young managers tend to have lots of toys—cool cell phones, the newest PDAs, fast cars, and flat-screen TVs. Why? You probably are not putting a child through college, you make more money than your staff, and you may even live with your family.

Your older employees tend to be much more conservative about money. As stated earlier, they were indirectly affected by their parents, who experienced the Great Depression. Debt strikes fear in their hearts.

You, on the other hand, were brought up almost expecting to take on some debt for your college education. You may have started young with education loans. Even earlier than that, your parents may have given you a credit card so that you could buy gas and food. Boomers were probably working for several years before acquiring a credit card and they are more cautious as a group about actually carrying the debt over from month to month.

This gulf in attitudes toward debt makes the generations look at risk in the workplace differently. You may make fast decisions regarding where and when to invest money and time and other resources. Boomers tend to want to do lengthier risk/reward analyses. This can lead to conflict when you are trying to move forward and lead your team on a new project.

Calming the Fears Regarding Risk

To mitigate fear, ask your Boomer to list all the risks that concern him and address each one briefly. Then ask him to list all the risks that could come with not moving forward. Discuss those and tell him that these are your concerns.

Secondly, ask the Boomer to try to think of a risk in the past five years in your company or department that paid off. This risk could be one of the following:

- A change in the way of processing something
- A new way to communicate with each other or customers
- A new material or vendor
- An addition to the product line or list of services offered

When she makes her list, ask her what the company/department would have lost if this change had not been made. Bring her to the realization that not taking a risk is a risk itself.

Younger workers are, in general, greater risk-takers and more entrepreneurial in style. As seen in Stephanie Armour's "Generation Y: They've Arrived at Work with a New Attitude":

> *"Generation Y is much less likely to respond to the traditional command-and-control type of management still popular in much of today's workforce," says Jordan Kaplan, an associate managerial science professor at Long Island University-Brooklyn in New York. "They've grown up questioning their parents, and now they're questioning their employers. They don't know how to shut up, which is great, but that's aggravating to the 50-year-old manager who says, Do it and do it now."*
>
> *That speak-your-mind philosophy makes sense to Katie Patterson, an assistant account executive at Edelman Public Relations in Atlanta. "We are willing and not afraid to challenge the status quo," she says. "An environment where creativity and independent thinking are looked upon as a*

the person to try it my way, and if that doesn't work try it their way.

- Treat everyone the same.
- As mentioned, older workers can sometimes be a little intimidated by a younger person who is an authority figure; they sometimes feel threatened by their positions.
- I find mutual respect goes a long way.
- I treat them with the respect they deserve and treat them like I would treat my grandmother.
- I think overall the biggest challenge is to ensure older employees receive the respect they are due based on their knowledge, while implementing new techniques and strategies that may not be embraced by older employees. I have found creating an atmosphere that expresses a partnership rather than a hierarchy of manager/subordinate is successful.
- Managers need to value the experiences and opinions of older workers.
- It's important to be respectful of the amount of knowledge and experience individuals have, and to be open to different viewpoints, regardless of someone's age. I don't hire or assess people based on their age, but on their skills, personality, and ability to work collaboratively.

Dos and Don'ts

Do be prepared to show you know your job and you are prepared and professional.

Do expect there to be issues of respect and don't let them catch you off guard or cause you to be defensive.

Do create partnerships and demonstrate that you value their experience and knowledge.

the risks that could come with not moving forward. Discuss those and tell him that these are your concerns.

Secondly, ask the Boomer to try to think of a risk in the past five years in your company or department that paid off. This risk could be one of the following:

- A change in the way of processing something
- A new way to communicate with each other or customers
- A new material or vendor
- An addition to the product line or list of services offered

When she makes her list, ask her what the company/department would have lost if this change had not been made. Bring her to the realization that not taking a risk is a risk itself.

Younger workers are, in general, greater risk-takers and more entrepreneurial in style. As seen in Stephanie Armour's "Generation Y: They've Arrived at Work with a New Attitude":

"Generation Y is much less likely to respond to the traditional command-and-control type of management still popular in much of today's workforce," says Jordan Kaplan, an associate managerial science professor at Long Island University-Brooklyn in New York. "They've grown up questioning their parents, and now they're questioning their employers. They don't know how to shut up, which is great, but that's aggravating to the 50-year-old manager who says, Do it and do it now."

That speak-your-mind philosophy makes sense to Katie Patterson, an assistant account executive at Edelman Public Relations in Atlanta. "We are willing and not afraid to challenge the status quo," she says. "An environment where creativity and independent thinking are looked upon as a

the person to try it my way, and if that doesn't work try it their way.

- Treat everyone the same.
- As mentioned, older workers can sometimes be a little intimidated by a younger person who is an authority figure; they sometimes feel threatened by their positions.
- I find mutual respect goes a long way.
- I treat them with the respect they deserve and treat them like I would treat my grandmother.
- I think overall the biggest challenge is to ensure older employees receive the respect they are due based on their knowledge, while implementing new techniques and strategies that may not be embraced by older employees. I have found creating an atmosphere that expresses a partnership rather than a hierarchy of manager/subordinate is successful.
- Managers need to value the experiences and opinions of older workers.
- It's important to be respectful of the amount of knowledge and experience individuals have, and to be open to different viewpoints, regardless of someone's age. I don't hire or assess people based on their age, but on their skills, personality, and ability to work collaboratively.

Dos and Don'ts

Do be prepared to show you know your job and you are prepared and professional.

Do expect there to be issues of respect and don't let them catch you off guard or cause you to be defensive.

Do create partnerships and demonstrate that you value their experience and knowledge.

- Don't speak down to them ever; they are still your elders. Don't try to come across as better than they are. If you talk to them like equals, I have found you will get more respect.

- I have found that working with older people can be very beneficial. I think the key is earning their respect, mostly just by showing them that you know what you are doing. I think it also helps to show that you appreciate their experience and ask for input often. The biggest mistake you can make is not knowing your own job. If they feel like they have to train you in everything you will always have a problem.

- Let them know that you don't know everything and are willing to listen to them.

- The best thing about older folks is they have respect for everyone and are willing to listen and try things a new way and are not so quick tempered like younger people. When you can sit down and talk things out, the problem is just about solved.

- I have found that older workers give me more respect and pay more attention to what I say.

Gen X and Y managers were also open to sharing what they have done in order to gain the trust and respect of their Boomer reports.

- Coach them without sounding condescending. Show them the respect they deserve while still managing them.

- In my experience, I've found that if I treat the older worker with respect, the other employees will also. I don't let anyone's age affect how I deal with that person; it's better to keep it about job performance.

- The challenge is showing them respect while giving instructions. I find it easy to hear their opinions and ask

the person to try it my way, and if that doesn't work try it their way.

- Treat everyone the same.
- As mentioned, older workers can sometimes be a little intimidated by a younger person who is an authority figure; they sometimes feel threatened by their positions.
- I find mutual respect goes a long way.
- I treat them with the respect they deserve and treat them like I would treat my grandmother.
- I think overall the biggest challenge is to ensure older employees receive the respect they are due based on their knowledge, while implementing new techniques and strategies that may not be embraced by older employees. I have found creating an atmosphere that expresses a partnership rather than a hierarchy of manager/subordinate is successful.
- Managers need to value the experiences and opinions of older workers.
- It's important to be respectful of the amount of knowledge and experience individuals have, and to be open to different viewpoints, regardless of someone's age. I don't hire or assess people based on their age, but on their skills, personality, and ability to work collaboratively.

Dos and Don'ts

Do be prepared to show you know your job and you are prepared and professional.

Do expect there to be issues of respect and don't let them catch you off guard or cause you to be defensive.

Do create partnerships and demonstrate that you value their experience and knowledge.

Don't talk down to them. To get respect you must first give respect.

Do be open to compromise—even though you are the boss and have the authority. You will gain more respect through collaboration.

Do be honest and communicate but always maintain that you are the manager and the ultimate decision-maker.

Don't let a condescending tone enter into your coaching of older workers.

Don't be surprised if your older employees treat you with more respect than your younger employees.

Do listen respectfully before speaking, managing, or coaching.

CHAPTER 8

Diversity in a Four-Generation Workplace

A management epiphany: Your diversity experience differs greatly from your older employee's experience.

No one had to teach you about diversity, but they did anyway. Statistically, it is extremely rare to find anyone in Generations X or Y who associates only with people of his race and ethnicity. You have lived diversity as you have sat side-by-side with the huge influx of immigrants from Mexico, eastern Europe, the Pacific Rim, and elsewhere. These faces and voices and cultures were familiar to you as early as kindergarten, or even before you started school. Of course, you value their intelligence, talents, and contributions. Why would you not?

But just in case you did miss the obvious during your childhood and adolescence, diversity was incorporated into your social studies, English, and other curriculums. Your principal participated in programs to incorporate diversity into assemblies, announcements, and other programs. Enough already. You get it.

On the other hand, most Boomers had to learn about diversity second hand. They have been extremely open to diversity, but they did not experience the diversity immersion therapy you did. In their childhoods, they may have associated only with people who looked like them and their parents. Their first workplaces were probably populated by people of their own race and ethnicity. Their first experience of working with another race may have been when someone was hired from the outside to add much-needed diversity to their company's management ranks. The job a minority took may have been one a Boomer always thought he or his close friend would be given. These are difficult circumstances under which to learn diversity.

Generation Y is the most diverse generation in U.S. history, with only 61 percent identifying themselves as "Caucasian." The generation's social circles are also the most diverse in recent history in relation to religion and race. A current study states that only 7 percent of this generation indicates that all of their friends are of the same race or religion.

Generation Y is considered more progressive than older generations on social issues, yet has a lower interest in politics than the generations ahead of it.

—*Anna Greenberg,*
"How Generation Y Is Redefining Faith in the iPod Era"

And diversity cuts both ways. Minority Boomers, just like those in the majority, have been influenced by parents and grandparents from a totally different era of workplace dynamics. Yet Boomers ushered in the boldest advances in diversity of any generation in the workplace. The diversity that Generation X and Y enjoy today was made possible by radical changes launched and supported by the Boomers. They were the change visionaries, the change agents, and the change implementers that transformed management ranks from the old white man's club to the rich and variegated consortium it is today. To the credit of the Boomers, the ones I talk to today are extremely supportive of even the changes brought into the workplace by mandates. All agree the changes were much needed and overdue. The Boomers may not have been born into a culture of diversity, but they gave birth to the multicultural workplace of today.

Still, diversity is not in their corporate DNA as it is in yours. They sometimes have to think through things a minute longer to recalibrate their years of experience to adapt to the workplace of today. They may start with an ingrained vision of what a person in a particular role might look like—like a male, like someone their age, or like Harrison Ford as the president in *Air Force One*. They are more than willing to change that view if their new manager is a twenty-seven-year-old Asian female, but give them a minute to adjust and take a breath.

Mentally, you don't have to go through these gyrations to adapt, but you need to allow time for your Boomer employees to do so. Many are unaware that only 61 percent of Generation Y is Caucasian, according to the 2000 U.S. Census. They may wonder why so many non-Caucasians are being hired into professional positions and believe the hiring is exclusionary to Caucasians. Good information and training can go a long way to updating the Boomer's understanding of hiring and succession planning practices. Be sure to provide your older employees with current statistics, articles, and successful case studies related to the diverse workplace.

And Boomers may need coaching and even formal training to update their outdated behaviors and attitudes related to diversity. Although not averse to the promotion of diverse coworkers, your Boomer manager may have unconscious prejudices or even outdated behaviors they may demonstrate in the workplace. One such behavior to note for males is open-ing doors for women and serving in the "protector" role that was required according to the business etiquette required of them in previous years. Similarly, they may attempt to be advi-sor and benign benefactor of wisdom to minorities, females, or younger employees. This generosity, with only the most noble intentions, may verge on paternalism or condescension.

Xerox is using the slogan "Express Yourself" as a way to describe its culture to recruits. The hope is that the slogan will appeal to Gen Y's desire to develop solutions and change. Recruiters also point out the importance of diversity at the company; Gen Y is one of the most diverse demographic groups—one out of three is a minority.

—Stephanie Armour,
"Generation Y: They've Arrived at Work with a New Attitude"

What can you do as a manager to aid a Boomer who may not be as fully acclimated to diversity as you are?

1. **As often as possible, pair the Boomer with the group (female, young, Hispanic, etc.) that is the most challenging for her.** Give the Boomer the role of the learner and the other employee the role of the teacher. In other words, send a Hispanic employee to the off-site training about a new product. Ask him to come back and teach the older employee about its features. The older employee may be the in-house expert on the legacy products, but she will see that she can learn from a Hispanic employee.

2. **Organize your workspace to give your Boomer employee day-to-day exposure to coworkers who are the most different from her.**

As a Gen-XYer, you had this exposure every day in school; your older employee probably did not. Some things are best learned by osmosis. Arrange desks to promote interaction and communication among all members of the team.

3. **Invest in on-site and off-site diversity training;** the experiential type is best.

4. **Finally, the most difficult but perhaps the most important strategy is to give the Boomer feedback in real time.** If the employee just assumes the Asian employee is strong in technology based on ethnicity, take the Boomer aside and let her know that her prejudice is showing. If the Boomer never allows the females sales reps to drive on calls, point this out. It is awkward to bring up these subtleties, but it is very constructive. You may want to bring up the point as a question: "Dave, do you remember in the meeting the other day when you said to John, 'Of course, I am sure you have an iPhone'? Did you say that because John is young? Asian?"

Pause here and let the employee fully discuss this from his point of view.

Decide if this is the time to reframe the situation for him by saying something like, "What if John said to you, 'David, I am sure you still have an eight-track tape player somewhere at home that you listen to.'" Prejudice can still cut both ways.

When Conflict Has Nothing to Do with Age

Recently, I was teaching business communication to a group of twenty-something businesspersons. As an icebreaker, I asked each person to introduce the person on his left. I overheard a young man begin the conversation with the young woman at his right, a person he had never met, with this shocking sentence:

"I'll bet you like to shop." This young woman was a driven and successful businessperson, already an entrepreneur at twenty-five. I doubt the young man would have begun a conversation with a male counterpart that way. Sometimes, a lack of sensitivity to inclusion has nothing to do with generation.

A diverse workplace means no discrimination up or down the generational ladder. You should have the same level of expectations for both older and younger workers. As discussed earlier, the most recent studies show that older workers tend to really value and respect their younger managers. One study that supports this claim is from the Family and Work Institute, a group funded by some of the nation's largest companies. Consider these findings from their article "The Generation Gap: More Myth Than Reality":

> *[Our] findings fly in the face of widely held beliefs that older workers tend to view their younger supervisors negatively—as having usurped their seniority, having robbed them of higher paying jobs, and lacking the experience to perform their jobs.*

So, in your efforts to develop diversity balance in your department, be sure you start with a nondiscriminatory attitude yourself toward the older worker. Not all discrimination relates to ethnicity and gender. Just as you would with any employee, assess the needs demonstrated by the older worker before judging that diversity coaching is needed.

The Successful Multigenerational Workplace

The Society for Human Resource Management's 2004 survey of 258 randomly selected HR professionals resulted in the following findings: Despite the prevalence of intergenerational work forces in every workplace, generational conflict is not widespread. Instead, organizations are reaping the benefits of the diversity provided by workers of different generations. Workers from different generations work effectively together and learn from one another. The most frequently reported problems are relatively minor and tend to stem from issues such as differing expectations regarding work hours and acceptable dress.

Thoughts on the Surprising Upside of Managing Older Workers

The following are actual comments related to the very positive experiences Gen-XYers are having as they manage older workers. There are perks and assets brought to the workplace through the older workers. All comments were written in by respondents to the XYBoom Survey. Only a representative sample of answers is included.

- My experience as a manager has been good. The older employees have a good work ethic and have not challenged me.
- Usually I don't have issues in dealing with older employees. Treating everyone as an equal, regardless of age or any other factor, seems to work best.
- I think any manager that has older workers needs to utilize the older workers' experience in life, not to mention in the business world: their patience and life experience can bring great experience to any project or team. They can level the playing field for competitors plus assist any manager in seeing potential in others.
- I have worked with an older person for four years and have found it to be a reward.
- They hold the team together.
- If the communication is open, I think managing older workers is beneficial to a company. They bring with them a wealth of knowledge that can help create better work environments for everyone.

- Older workers have an "idea" of what should be happening in a work environment that usually is different from what younger workers think.
- Over all I've never had any major problems with an older worker; they're always on time and do the job which they are given without a lot of back talk.
- They have valuable experience and need a forum for discussion.
- They can be set in their ways but usually have some valuable insights and contributions.
- Some of the older workers that I supervise do have a poor attitude about a younger supervisor, but others are genuinely a pleasure to work with. A lot of my older workers have had other careers before this one, such as engineering and accounting, that gives them a good background in any field for finding solutions to problems that arise.
- They have more experience, and combined with my knowledge we can come up with better ideas faster and easier.
- Older workers in my experience tend to be less organized but somehow manage to handle the disorganization. They are usually more patient about situations and somehow know that everything will work out in the end. They wait for conflicts to resolve themselves at times.
- They will keep generational problems between supervisors and employees at a minimum.
- I have had to devote additional training time and tutorials for these workers; however, I have been able to benefit from their vast work experiences. Younger managers need to understand what motivates the older worker and be sensitive to his/her needs. Young managers, can at times, demonstrate frustration.
- They are very conscientious, always on time, and always show up and do as they are told. They take pride in what they do.

- Older workers are an asset.

A finding from the XYBoom Survey is that many younger managers often actually prefer older workers to Generation X and Y employees.

- Overall I've found that older workers are much easier to work with than younger employees.
- They are smarter, better workers, dedicated, and easy to work with.
- Younger employees tend to have an attitude of entitlement.
- Working with older workers is better than working with young workers; they are more dependable and they work more. They have better work ethics.
- I believe that older workers are more dedicated to their jobs due to good work ethics. I feel the younger generation does not want to work.
- Older workers are more stable and show up for work; younger workers are unreliable and can't focus on tasks to get them done on time. I prefer older workers any day of the week.
- No challenge. Actually older workers are more dependable and open to learning something new.

However, some younger managers wrote in to say that they see prejudice against older workers in the workplace and the injustice is a concern to them.

- Sometimes they do not respect people older than them.
- There are situations where young managers do not value what older workers can bring to a business through their experience. I have also seen many situations where older workers that are established in a company have little or

no respect when newly hired or promoted managers are much younger then they are. Regardless of age, I believe that when new managers are brought onboard to supervise an established team, they need to show the employees why upper management hired them to "run the team" through their actions.

- The biggest challenge I see with younger people managing older workers is that the younger ones tend to have a know-it-all attitude and are unwilling to adjust for the older worker's skills and abilities.

- Younger managers in my company come into their management position and expect everyone to be on the same page as them. Some of the older workers who have been with the company twenty-plus years are having a harder time adapting to younger managers because of their expectations.

Dos and Don'ts

Do evaluate each person's ideas and performance based on merit and objective standards without regard to age.

Don't ignore the wisdom, warnings, and insight you can gain from them. They often know more than anyone in the company about your job and can be a valued asset to you.

Do foster an atmosphere of respect for older workers by demonstrating your own respect for the older workers. Serve as a model for any younger worker who may have a disrespectful attitude.

Don't ignore good advice just because the source is someone who reports to you.

Do capitalize on their diverse experience from other companies and even other fields they once worked in. This is rich and valuable insight that they have accumulated and that you can use.

Do state and demonstrate that there is no entitlement in your department, just earned rewards and recognition.

Do promote older employees without regard to the time remaining in their careers. Older workers often stay longer than younger workers who may job-hop and end up staying a shorter time than the employee close to retirement age.

Don't forget that older employees have many strengths. Use their expertise in areas where they are strong, like in being a team facilitator because they work well with all generations.

CHAPTER 9

Creativity, Innovation, Change, and Risk

In a recent *BusinessWeek* article about the top twenty rising twenty-five-and-under entrepreneurs, Ryan Pieter Middleton Allis of Broadwick Corporation offers this advice to his peers, younger managers like you:

> *I've learned to have a bias toward action in everything that I do. The second biggest lesson: Always keep your ear to the ground and integrate your customers into your product-development efforts.*

This bias toward action is part of the creative impulse that younger managers tend to give freer range than their older peers and employees. Another young entrepreneur and owner of a greeting-card business cited in the article, Joanna Albert, put it like this:

> *If something doesn't feel right, then I just shouldn't do it. I follow my gut.*

Taking the risk to follow one's gut is a pervasive value among younger generations. Although there are people in every generation who have done this, the risk-taking-follow-my-brainstorm kind of lifestyle is not common in older generations. Older employees tend to look to the past. In other words, they may try to see if an idea has a track record of success, documentation, or at least a major company that has tried the idea before. There is a healthy skepticism about being the first to do anything.

Generation X and Y managers, however, may see being the first to try something, though risky, as an exciting opportunity to do something fresh, new, and perhaps better than anything that has come before.

And there can be profit in doing things in fresh, new ways—so much profit that legacy businesses are trying to capture this young way of thinking.

Another young entrepreneur featured in *BusinessWeek*, Anand Chhatpar, has found a way to link traditional corporations with new ideas from younger thinking consumers. When asked to share a business lesson learned, Chhatpar said:

> *Think of scalability in everything you do, and leverage smart work. Innovative ideas come from fresh minds and exploring new perspectives, so don't jump to conventional wisdom. And remember Richard Branson's code: "Oh screw it, let's do it."*

This combination of valuing innovation and then trusting one's instincts to go with it is the hallmark of Generation Y. You may be thinking that it is also true of young people in general, no matter their generation. This is true, but the Internet and other communication tools have uniquely enabled the younger generations to take their ideas national, even global, relatively inexpensively and very, very fast. And advertising using the web can offer low cost avenues and huge numbers that entrepreneurs of previous generations could never have afforded as start-ups.

All this to say, your generations, X and Y, have received support and reinforcement for being innovative risk-takers that just were not there for Baby Boomers. And this gap makes a difference in the day-to-day way you manage older workers.

If your executive VP mandates you trash your traditional marketing plan in order to target clients and try something radically new, you may think, "Very cool. We may discover some new pockets of revenue and this will definitely be a change of pace. I was getting a bit bored with just knocking on the same doors all the time."

A Boomer is more likely to be very concerned about abandoning an approach that everyone for years has agreed was the most profitable approach. They may be concerned about their own ability to succeed with this new market, and being unsuccessful is scarier the older you get. Visions of a meager retirement or inability to help children with tuition play on the older worker's mind.

You see, it's not that the Boomers can't be innovative and creative; it's that they have been taught to put on the mental and psychological brakes every time a highly creative, outside the box idea comes along and to look for everything that can go wrong. You, on the other hand, have been thoroughly trained and encouraged to think outside the box and to pursue those innovative ideas. You have been encouraged to take chances and not to let risk stop you. Boomers were groomed to avoid risk for the first twenty years of their careers—at least.

So it is up to you, their manager, to give them the same training and encouragement that you received to be innovative, creative risk-takers. How do you do that?

1. Involve older workers in brainstorming sessions.
2. Be on the lookout for any suggestions from Boomers that might be new or creative. Reward this thinking immedi-

ately with affirmation, implementation of the idea, or in any way available to you.

3. Find ways to implement a contest or other way to generate and reward new ideas. Be sure you acknowledge and reinforce the ideas of the older workers.

4. Ask older workers to study competitors and allies to learn new ways other companies are improving products, services, or performance. Ask older workers to bring these ideas back to the department and share them with others.

5. Ask older workers to survey or interview customers to get new ideas for how to improve your service and products.

6. Ask older workers to survey peers to make two lists: a list of the services and product features customers like best and a list of the most common complaints. Furnish them with any research or information you have on this. Then, ask them to study the list and make some suggestions. How can you improve your products and services to strengthen the best features and improve on the complaint areas. Perhaps you could let older workers lead a brainstornming session on this topic.

7. Assign older workers to read and study about entrepreneurs, risk-takers, and creativity in business during regular work hours. They need to understand that you consider innovation and creativity to be hard business assets. Search in your field under creativity and entrepreneurship.

8. Many seminars are available on creative problem-solving, risk-taking, and entrepreneurship. Sign up older workers.

Above all, encourage older workers to be creative and innovative. Give them permission to fail at first while they are taking risks. As Ryan Hudson of Youshoot.com, another young entrepreneur featured in *BusinessWeek*, says, "You just have to do it sometimes, and you'll figure it out later."

Hiring for Creativity and Innovation

When you hire people, do you give an edge to people who are innovators? Those who approach projects creatively? Who are willing to take a risk? Who can deal with almost constant change? Some or all of these are probably true of you if you are a Generation X or Y manager. These are survival skills in today's workplace.

Not so when the Boomers started their careers. In fact, *risk* was a bad word in business. Hiring managers steered clear if someone seemed a little too open to change. Changing careers three times by thirty was grounds for suspicion that something was very wrong with a job candidate. And there was no need for innovation unless you were in advertising or R & D.

Considering their background, Boomers have come a long way. They have learned to be more flexible than they ever dreamed they could be. They certainly thought no one would ever ask them to be so adaptable to change. Still, innovation and risk are not inherent in the background of a Boomer as it is in yours. As stated above, these concepts are part of your expectation of the workplace and were stressed in your colleges, high schools, and even kindergartens. Boomers were still dealing with more concrete topics.

Make sure your Boomer managers are including innovation, risk-taking, and creative problem-solving on their list of criteria for new hires. These strengths will be necessary for the work force of the future.

Managing by Objective Versus Managing for Innovation

For many years, management by objective (MBO) ruled business and industry. MBO means that executives and managers devise goals, set a timeline, and communicate expectations. Employees just do it, lockstep. The objective should not change if the employee falls behind on the timeline. The goal rarely changed even if the executives began to wonder if it was even a good one. The company usually considered it to be a failure if an objective, once stated, was ever delayed or abandoned or amended. The solution was that the employees had to work harder to force the project to a conclusion that fit with the original objective, even if it no longer fit the business plan. Although MBO has been modified to accommodate the changing workplace, it is the old version that struck fear in the hearts of older workers—fear of changing anything committed to, fear of new tasks not on the work plan, and fear of taking new risks.

Although setting targets is an excellent idea for boosting performance, you should always remind employees that the communication lines are open if anyone sees a need for change. Clearly stating that you want everyone on the team to come to you if he or she sees a need to alter objectives is the first step. Second, you should take the initiative to communicate with older workers individually on a periodic basis. Ask about any progress toward an objective and whether the goal is still realistic. Ask about the timeline and what you can do to help the employee be successful. You may have to do this for a while, because older workers may not be used to this type of collaborative management style. Teach older workers that you really do want to incorporate their ideas into your decisions and that you value the collaboration.

Vigilant for Innovation

The old-school path to success was to improve upon what you found in a company you joined. Today's workplace demands we not just improve but find fresh ideas and entirely new products, services, and applications. It is our job to invent new processes and to create markets where there were none before. These ideas must be taught to Boomers just the way software applications are taught.

In the workplace the Boomers grew up in, if you joined a company that made tin cans, you were successful if you could find ways for the company to make more tin cans per hour or if you could make a better-quality can. These are still viable business goals, but to be really successful today, Boomers must understand that they have to innovate beyond that narrow goal. Employees today need to be asking, "Is there another product besides the tin can that we should be making as well? Are there uses of the tin can in medicine, automotives, and other markets that we have never explored? Should we even be in the tin can business?"

Ask Nokia if this is a winning business strategy. After years of producing plastic pipe and ho-hum sales, they used their plastics expertise to make cell phones. The explosive growth and profits of Nokia are the type of success story every company is seeking today. Your Boomer employees, with their wealth of general business experience, might just be the ones who can see an application for your product or services that could boost profits. It is your job as their leader to show them how to innovate and bring forward their creativity.

As suggested, nothing is more effective in encouraging this innovative, risk-taking thinking than rewards. You see, deep in his heart, the Boomer really thinks there is a punishment waiting for him at the end of a risk. You can't just give pep talks about innovation and risk. You must reward every tiny hint of creativity and innovation you see in the Boomer's work or conversation.

Great ideas and possibilities are just as likely to be discovered by a Boomer as a younger worker if you train the Boomer to be on the lookout for ways to innovate. As twenty-five-year-old entrepreneur Ejovi Nuwere, founder of SecurityLab Technologies, said in his *Business Week* interview, "Opportunity is everywhere, if you're only willing to see it."

Thoughts on Abandoning Old Mindsets, Leading Positive Change, and Encouraging Creativity, Innovation, and Appropriate Risk

The following are actual comments related to change, creativity, and appropriate risks that were written in by respondents to the XYBoom Survey. Only a representative sample of answers is included.

According to the XYBoom Survey, some older workers just don't like change and are not very flexible.

- Getting them to change old work habits is a challenge.
- They are more stubborn and set in their ways; it is harder to get them to accept change. I have one guy who will simply decide that he isn't going to do something if he thinks it's too much.
- The biggest challenge I've faced is when an older worker thought that she had knowledge that she didn't. If I asked her to do something a different way, that I thought would be better and more efficient, she would passive-aggressively do it the same way.
- Sometimes I have to deal with less-flexible workers, and they tend to be older workers.
- The older workers feel they know exactly how everything should be done and do not ask about the appropriate way to do something in the current company they work for.
- My problem is that sometimes they are not as open-minded, and they are set in their ways. They are resistant to change, open communication, and they value old ways and opinions.
- Lots of times they are set in their ways and think they have only one job to do. In my line of work, we do numerous types of jobs.

- Older workers have a tendency to rely on what's worked in the past rather than exploring new, better options.
- Older workers have a harder time changing. When there is a change in processes/procedures/technology, they are always the ones who have the hardest time adjusting to the change.
- They are so easily upset by change. They like to do things the way they've always done them, and they don't want to listen to explanations about why certain things are necessary. I had one lady threaten to quit if she had to take a customer service test. She said people should just "do right" and "let people be." Well, of course, that's true, but in today's corporate climate, we have to show compliance with certain things, and ethics and customer service training is part of that.
- Older employees are unable to adapt quickly and think outside the box.

As evidenced by the following responses, some older workers demonstrate a know-it-all attitude, believing that just because they are older they are wiser than their younger managers.

- Some older workers believe they've "seen it all." When an idea is presented, they say the company tried that twenty years ago and it didn't work. I've had to remind them that a lot has changed since the last time the idea was tried. We need to evaluate ideas on their merits based on today's environment, rather than assume it won't work because it didn't work before.
- I think the hardest thing for a lot of younger managers to overcome is that you can't talk to the older guys like you can the younger ones. If you show them that you respect them, they are usually extremely loyal and willing to go above and beyond for you.

- Older workers don't always want to listen to younger managers and will stick to their stubborn "my way is the best way" attitude.
- My biggest challenge has been that older workers don't take me seriously.
- They are set in their ways and are hard to adapt to innovative or modern ways of doing things. They feel they already know everything.
- The biggest challenge has been just attitude. They are "set in their ways."

Many young managers wrote in to share the numerous ways that any issues of clinging to old ways could be easily overcome. The solutions are diverse and many, minimizing barriers to flexibility and change.

- Many older employees have an old way of thinking. They prefer face to face and they believe someone should pay their dues before they are promoted. They want to see that you can do the job they are doing and prefer praise for work done well.
- One worker was very set in her ways and could not understand why she was not getting the results the other reps were. I asked her and another successful rep to go on ride-alongs together—one day in the older rep's territory, the next day in the younger rep's area. They both learned valuable new ideas from each other.
- I find older workers have a harder time adapting to change at the workplace. I try to help them adapt to the changing environment with face-to-face discussions about their concerns with what is going to change. Younger managers in my company come into their management position and expect everyone to be on the same page as younger employees.

- The biggest challenge is older workers who want to do something "the way we used to do it." What I propose is a slight variation that would provide me with all the data I need and then I make any final adjustments.
- I work in a very fast-paced emergency services department. Most of the people I work with or supervise that are older than me began in this field at a much younger age and are able to adjust with each change, but if an older person is hired in without previous experience, the job's demands are too great for them to keep up. It makes them feel insecure and obsolete. Truthfully, regardless of managing techniques, hiring older workers in my field does not work well.
- Normally we have to have a sit-down conversation one on one and discuss issues we have before we can move forward. Everyone has his or her own ideas to share, and it doesn't matter whether you're twenty or eighty: you can still participate as well as anyone else.
- Older employees are reluctant to learn new procedures. They need to be shown in small increments for better results.
- It is difficult to counsel older employees while maintaining a balance of respect and effective coaching.
- Some types of older workers are rigid and stubborn. I tackle such situations many times by exhibiting understanding.
- Some of them are slow, set in their ways, and stubborn. However, they are knowledgeable and reliable. You have to find the right balance. In my experience, setting up reward systems makes them feel that they are being condescended to.
- I treat them with respect and patience and have really enjoyed the older people who work for me. I spend a lot of time with my grandmother, so that is where I get most of my ideas of how to treat these people. If I try to tell them

what to do forcefully they just think I am being a bossy "upstart." If I tell them what I would like to be done and why and listen to their input, they are much more likely to do what needs to be done. I also have learned to be flexible and let them work at their pace and in their way when possible, as long as I get the same results.

- When training new employees with old standards, I tell them, "I think it's great that you did it that way at your old location, but this way is much more efficient; but if you can show us a way to be more efficient than this way, I am more than open to the idea." I like to give them some "control" so that they don't feel trapped by our ways and therefore don't show this new employee that we are not "set" in our ways either.
- You have to show them why a new way may be better.
- Younger managers have to earn the respect and loyalty of older managers without losing authority.
- If you can motivate them to set goals and help them to achieve goals by using out-of-the box techniques, they tend to want to learn.

Young managers wrote in frequently to say they simply did not experience any problems with older workers adapting to changes or new ways of doing things.

- It really depends on the person. Most older people are set in their ways, but on the other hand, younger people are not as reliable at times.
- Personally, I have no problems with older workers. I have seen younger managers who have less patience when dealing with older workers who are slower, or those who have been doing the job for many years though not in the same way the younger ones would do it.

- If the communication is open, I think managing older workers is beneficial to a company. They bring with them a wealth of knowledge that can help create better work environments for everyone.

Dos and Don'ts

Do find out what the individual motivators are for each employee and approach change with the idea of motivating the employee to desire to support the change.

Do listen to the older employee's ideas for how to implement processes and procedures. Occasionally, they are right. If not, they still will be more invested in change if they feel you listened.

Don't always assume the issue is age. Everyone has different ideas, no matter the age. Keep an open mind.

Don't invest time in issues that are really not long-term problems. Is it really a problem that this employee took two weeks to be proficient at a new process while your younger employee took only a week? If at the end of two weeks all employees are fully functioning, do you really need to invest time in pointing out that it took the older worker twice as long? Choose your battles.

Do reward even the tiniest step toward innovation and creativity.

Do expose older workers to new industry trends and ideas through conferences, seminars, and trade shows.

Do take it slow when introducing new processes. Teach change in small increments.

Do have sit-down, face-to-face meetings with older employees when you are introducing change. Just whipping out an e-mail or text message will not give the employee a chance to vent any initial fears and frustrations; they will come out in other ways, perhaps in passive-aggressive noncompliance.

Do expect to demonstrate your competence and to earn an older worker's respect before she respects your leadership in change.

Do read Chapter 5 to maintain great communication for the long term.

Don't let changes and new procedures pile up. Change is more difficult if there is a lot to relearn all at once. Help older workers keep up with incremental changes. Younger workers generally play with new ideas and technologies as they go along, because the new stuff is interesting, and Gen-XYers like to play with new technologies and new ideas. Older workers tend not to play around with new ideas or technologies. Give the older worker time to experiment with anything new as it comes up.

CHAPTER 10

What Generations X and Y Managers Need to Learn from the Boomers

The XYBoom Survey delivered proof positive of the caring nature of Generations X and Y. Over and over again, the responding younger managers communicated the great regard and appreciation they have for the Baby Boomers. Still, as Boomers retire at an accelerated rate in this decade, I don't think any of us is prepared for how the landscape of our workplace is about to change. Some phrases come to mind:

- You don't know what you've got till it's gone.
- Experience is the best teacher.
- There is no substitute for experience.

On January 1, 2008, the oldest of the Baby Boomer pack reached the traditional retirement age of sixty-two. Over the next twenty years, 77 million will exit the workplace. If nothing is done to garner the wisdom, experience, and strengths of that generation, a void will be left in some strategic areas that they now fill. We tend to take for granted their stability, endurance, and accountability. The XYBoom Survey respondents commented time after time that they depend on their older workers for this stability and responsibility to offset these areas of weakness in their younger employees. With that balance missing, what will happen to productivity, performance, and our standing in international markets?

The solution is to begin to assimilate all that is of value from the Baby Boomer work ethos and experience. The following section explores the six areas of skill and expertise younger employees should attempt to learn from older employees before the Boomers retire. Generations X and Y should be in hot pursuit to grab all the rich assets that this older generation can bequeath to them. Consider each acquisition of knowledge and experience from the Boomers a target to aim for. Pursue these learning targets that have been identified as particularly valuable to retain for the future:

Learning Target 1: Social skills and building social capital
Learning Target 2: Negotiating skills
Learning Target 3: Nonverbal communication
Learning Target 4: Critical and strategic thinking
Learning Target 5: Career endurance and investment
Learning Target 6: Personal accountability

Learning Target 1: Social Skills and Building Social Capital

Social fluency is not just a communication and management issue but an issue that will affect whether your company is effective in the global marketplace. The ability to build social capital has some hard dollar consequences and rewards attached.

Although, as mentioned in Chapter 6, Generation Y considers itself to be the relational generation, that reputation is largely based on the number of times they contact friends and coworkers and not on the skills demonstrated in relating on a personal or social level. Generation X has an even greater reputation for disregarding traditional social skills for a variety of reasons.

How Did Social Skills Decline after the Boomer Generation?

Generation X was the first generation to grow up looking at screens: computer screens, caller ID, text messages, and so on. By the time Generation Y came along, they were practically born with a cell phone in hand and watching constantly for instant messages on the family computer. The first social skill to go was eye contact.

When Gen-XYers decided it was acceptable to hold a conversation while keeping their eyes glued on a screen or while even text messaging, something was lost in interpersonal connection and social skills. Answers to questions got briefer and more terse. When eyes did not connect, a deeper connection was lost. Real engagement and thoughtful interest in conversations with others diminished.

You may consider relationship building a soft skill, but there are some hard business realities to consider as well. Developing and motivating people starts with communicating with them authentically and personally. Every great manager knows that you have to invest in people and genuinely get to know their aspirations and values before you can get amazing performance from them. This is hard to do when you don't stop the noise and distractions and devote dedicated time away from electronics to focus on others.

Think of the Boomers who have motivated or mentored you. Think of those who really made an impact on your life. In most cases, you will think of a time they really listened to you or conversed with you without the look or demeanor of being distracted by other calls or messages. It felt good. Employees, regardless of generation, need this investment of authentic interest.

Gen-XYers have taught the business world a lot about improving productivity through multitasking. We will never return to the wasteful practices of large meetings that can be accomplished by e-mails or unnecessary and frequent face-to-face communication when an instant message is more efficient. Still, when it comes to social skills, there is much to be learned from the Boomers.

Another social skill that should be salvaged is the practice of following up with notes or compliments. Ken Blanchard talks about "catching people doing something right" in his book *The One Minute Manager*. Boomers are great at this. They may even send a thank-you note on real paper. Ask anyone how memorable a thank-you note has been to them compared to an e-mail and you will quickly understand that there is real value in this practice.

Employees need touch points of remembrance to celebrate good things that happen in the workplace. You will always be motivated to point out the errors and behaviors that need to be corrected. The courteous practices and etiquette of the Boomer generation mandated that people also note and congratulate one another on achievements, promotions, successes, and advances. These courtesies had some positive residual effects on the workplace and on workers.

Basic courtesies should also be reviewed so that you can retain the most valuable practices. There is value in knowing how to execute a proper introduction, because the need for those comes up often in the workplace. Internationally, these skills are critical. Having a form or format for anything takes the quandary and inefficiency out of it. There are great formats for introductions and many other situations that will make you more polished and confident, because you know exactly what you are doing.

Learning to reciprocate when invited to lunch or to other events will build your network; failing to do so can hurt your career. Again, most of these basic courtesies are not just empty practices; they are based on being thoughtful of others. People who spend time and other resources showing you hospitality will wonder why you don't send a note or reciprocate. Basic consideration is the underlying reason behind thank-you notes and the etiquette rules of reciprocation. Failing to perform these basic courtesies can close doors and hurt business relationships that could prove valuable to you.

Many Baby Boomers are great at teaching these basics. You will notice that they will include more "pleases" and "thank-yous" in their everyday communication. They have more sensitive antennae to notice when someone needs a door opened or help with carrying things. This hyper-awareness was ingrained in them and was called common courtesy. This level of courtesy is in danger of being lost if we don't look up from our text messages long enough to learn this thoughtful work style that makes everyone feel better and the workplace more pleasant.

The final reason to aim for this learning target is that there is financial value in social capital. Tamer Cavusgil, an elected Fellow of International Business, said in a meeting at Georgia State University recently that one of the most valuable assets any company can acquire going into this global economy is social capital and the ability to build relations with other countries and other companies.

While he was delivering his presentation, an ambassador to a South American country popped in for a moment to say hello. Without knowing the topic under discussion, the ambassador said, "Tell your students that they must learn to develop relationships. Social capital is what we need to improve our import-export balance and strengthen our role in the international marketplace. It is all about relationships."

Becoming more relational and learning the nonverbal and other skills that are prized in certain cultures isn't just being a nice guy; these assets have tremendous value in your career and to your company.

How to Achieve This Target

1. **Observing and assimilating are the most effective ways to absorb social skills.** Be sure you spend some time around older workers to learn their style of handling people and situations.

2. **Ask a Boomer what courtesies or rules of etiquette have eroded in his view.** Ask him if he thinks they are worthwhile to your business. This discussion will serve two purposes. First, the Boomer may have some great learning points for you. Second, you have demonstrated an interest in social skills that may open up an ongoing dialogue on this subject. The Boomer may feel freer to comment on courteous acts or the lack thereof in the future.

3. **Etiquette books and other media abound.** Use these for yourself or as the basis of a discussion for your staff.

Learning Target 2: Negotiating Skills

No generation before has achieved the negotiating finesse that the Baby Boomers have developed. If we do not learn from them, no generation after them will derive the benefit of what they have learned. Boomers have taken the cruder skills of previous generations and turned negotiating into an art form.

Closely related to social skills, negotiating requires great skill to enable managers to be assertive about what their department or company needs or wants while maintaining a good relationship with the vendors, other departments, or customers. Baby Boomers invented the concept of win-win and are very good at it.

Why Boomers Are the Best Negotiators

Boomers are better than previous generations like the Traditionalists for several reasons. They are the first generation not to be shackled by false modesty and outmoded etiquette that prevented previous generations from touting the strength of their positions. Boomers had many new experiences that their parents never had. Many were the first in their families to go to college; they may have been the first to fly, travel internationally, and achieve a high-level position in a large company. Because they had to make their way, they are more aggressive than their parents and this serves them well in profitable negotiations.

Yet they have not lost the polite approach to negotiating conversations that their parents taught them. They have learned which rules to keep and which are a hindrance in a negotiation. For instance, Boomers are far more likely to boast of the strengths of their products or positions in a negotiation than their parents were. This positioning of what your strengths are is just good business and clear communication. A Boomer will politely acknowledge the strengths of an adversary but is not shy about saying why his product is better.

Boomers also had to be scrappier than Generations X and Y, so they are not afraid of a good tussle. Boomers had to fight for much of what they earned in the evolving workplace they experienced. These challenges made them more assertive in going for a goal. With the philosophy that everyone is a winner that most Gen-XYers grew up in, it is difficult for younger workers to be as motivated to exploit their edge over a competitor or internal negotiating partner. Some of this passion to win is strong fuel to make a negotiator more effective, so consider seeing if the Boomers can pass on some of this fire-in-the-belly before they are out of your life.

How to Achieve This Target

1. **Ask a Boomer to handle a negotiation for you.** Request that she make this a learning experience for you. Ask for a premeeting to see how she preps and what her strategy is. Observe her closely during negotiations to see specific things she says and does. Note how she starts the conversation and

what she does when rebuffed. If possible, observe several negotiations, as the Boomer may use different approaches with different personalities and situations.

2. **Attend many of the fine negotiating seminars developed by this generation.** Executive Speaker has an excellent one.

3. **Ask the Boomer to try to give you a list of recommendations he has for negotiating.** Tell him he can deliver it in the way most comfortable for him: e-mail, a casual conversation, or a presentation.

Learning Target 3: Nonverbal Communication

Studies show that nonverbal communication is three to five times more powerful than the verbal messages. If the skills to send and discern nonverbal messages are so powerful, shouldn't you want to develop them? You should know that Baby Boomers are the best at sending and receiving nonverbal messages. Generations X and Y—not so much. For all the reasons mentioned in the communications chapters, younger workers have not acquired the highly developed nonverbal communication abilities of the Boomers.

And if you think that the emphasis on nonverbal communication as a management skill is exaggerated, just think about this: What if you went into a meeting of your staff and looked down at the floor and failed to establish eye contact. You squirmed and slouched and looked uncomfortable. Then you said, "Corporate has changed your health benefits and I think it is going to be better and you have nothing to be concerned about." The verbal message is that all is well. The nonverbal message is that something is wrong. Employees will believe the nonverbal message over the verbal message every time. You must learn to develop positive nonverbals that are appropriate to your message.

Not only should you learn these skills for employee management but for your own career management. The impression that interviewers get of you when you are interviewing for a job is largely a feeling or a sense of who you are. Much of this impression is nonverbal. Sending nonverbal messages that you are confident but not arrogant, relaxed but not passive, and engaged but not too aggressive is key to interview success.

In short, strong nonverbal communication skills are valuable in every facet of your career, and the Boomers are the masters of nonverbal communication.

How to Achieve This Target

1. **Observe a variety of Boomers as they converse. Note how animated they are compared to more laid back, younger employees.** Pay attention to what their eyebrows, mouths, and eyes are doing as they express interest, surprise, affirmation, and concern. Also note posture and hand gestures.

2. **Pay special attention to the gestures and expressions Boomers use when making presentations.** Decide which ones would work for you and experiment with them.

3. **Develop facial expressions to go along with the following words:** "Congratulations," "Sorry," "Really?" "Thank you," "I'm listening," and "I agree." Also develop your Mona Lisa smile, a pleasant look to use when your face is in neutral, because your face is never in neutral.

4. **Practice the expressions above in a mirror until you have perfected them.**

Learning Target 4: Critical and Strategic Thinking

Internet skills strengthen younger employees' ability to react immediately, communicate in real time, and deploy resources instantly. Unfortunately, these strengths are being substituted for critical and strategic thinking. The best managers will develop strengths in both areas.

Older workers are best at pausing a moment and assimilating all the facts, weighing the possible outcomes of various choices, and developing the best strategic response. If older employees spend too much time on this stage it leads to analysis paralysis, but a bit of strategic thinking is valuable. Mentally bringing together the needs of all stakeholders and evaluating resources before shooting off instant messages has a place in a manager's skill set.

Looking at the domino effect of decisions is another component of critical thinking. Younger employees can learn from the more cautious and studied approach of older workers, though it is important not to diminish the Gen-XYers tolerance for risk. Many decisions affect the interdependent relationships within a company and with other stakeholders, and Boomers are stronger at being evaluative about the outcomes of actions that affect this interdependence.

How to Achieve This Target

1. Interview three Boomers and ask the following questions:

A. Tell about a time you had to think strategically before making a decision. What were all the people and conditions you had to consider. In retrospect, what would you have done differently?

B. What was the most far-thinking decision you made or what was a decision you made because it was a good long-term move?

C. What long-term or strategic elements may be neglected in the current way of doing business in the future as Boomers retire?

2. **Local colleges offer courses in strategic thinking, logic, and strategic management.** Consider taking a graduate or undergraduate class.
3. **Ask a Boomer senior manager or executive to give you an example of good business strategy or critical thinking that he has observed in his career.**

Learning Target 5: Career Endurance and Investment

Paying dues. Climbing the ladder. Waiting for good things to come. Patience is a virtue. All of these are Boomer concepts that Generation X and Y are not rushing to embrace. And in some instances, the waiting and the dues-paying have kept some Boomers from taking risks they should have, so younger managers have a point in not buying in to this philosophy completely. Also, from the moment Bill Gates dropped out of college and started the phenomena called Microsoft, becoming the billionaire extraordinaire, Generation X has had a poster boy for not climbing the ladder in the traditional way.

The truth is that most careers do not follow the flaming trajectory that Gates has. You will need to work out your own path of calculated risk and, yes, a bit of dues paying. Boomers are great sources of wisdom when it comes to long-term career planning. They have watched many careers and have learned a lot from the winners and from the losers. They have been surprised by some career moves that worked despite going against conventional wisdom and they have seen bad moves result in everyone saying, "I told you so." As sounding boards about career-related moves, there is no one who can help you more than the Boomers.

I say sounding board because past experience is all the Boomers can offer. We are in a very different job market that requires risk. Listening to their advice and being open to amending your plans is recommended; conducting your career exactly as they have is not. Things are just moving too fast today and the high rate of change in jobs and opportunities is greater. Following are five things you can learn from a Boomer about demonstrating your professionalism and showing your company that you have a career and not just a job with them:

Boomers have demonstrated the perseverance to get up every day and go to a workplace that is going through a difficult time and is unpleasant. Despite the problems Boomers may face each day, they show up on time and their productivity is not diminished by the negative circumstances around them. They weather the bad times and know that these things are cyclical. There is a saying: "If you want a new job, stay where you are." As workplaces change, management changes, and the economy changes; Boomers know that in all probability this too shall pass.

Boomers are better at not discussing the frustrations and negativity related to trivial or temporary circumstances. Although communicating problems is a good thing, people who rehash the obvious problems or complain about every little thing rarely advance far as leaders.

Boomers have learned the art of office politics. If they are not happy with workplace circumstances, they are more skillful at working with management and peers to tweak the existing situation. They are more apt to stay and work at it than to abandon this workplace for another. They have also been around the block enough to know that the new workplace they will go to has its problems too. They have probably had the experience of leaving one position for another with worse management and worse problems. Experience really is the best teacher on this one. Learn from the Boomer's experience instead of losing costly time finding it out for yourself.

Boomers can do what Stephen R. Covey in *The 7 Habits of Highly Effective People* recommends: "Begin with the end in mind." They were brought up to look at very long-term success targets. Generation X and Y were raised to focus more on short-term targets. Boomers can better visualize what a long-term goal can mean to them eventually in their finances and especially in their lifestyle. The comfort and ease that many Boomers are now experiencing in their late careers and in their retirement is their reward for the many dues they paid in their earlier careers. Boomers will tell you it was more than worth it.

Yet developing the appropriate degree of personal account-ability will distinguish you as a manager. The following section tells how to acquire the best parts of this trait.

How to Achieve This Target

1. **Interview three Boomers whose careers you admire. Ask them to tell you the following:**
   - A general synopsis of their career path
   - Early choices or decisions that worked out well
   - Investments of time or effort that paid off surprisingly well or that did not pay off as they had thought
   - What they would advise
   - What they would do differently
   - Consider asking them to mentor you or be a sponsor (an advocate who spends less time than a mentor but will help from time to time)

2. **Make a list of five things you could do that would be a good investment in your career** (learn a foreign language, earn another degree, work internationally, rotate to another part of the company, etc.). Ask a diverse group of people (friends, coworkers, executives) to rank them in the order of how valuable an investment they would be in your par-

ticular career—1 being highest and 5 being lowest. Ask conversationally why people think you should or should not do these items on your list. Consider the input and take a step toward investing in at least one of the items.

3. **Play with puzzles, Mensa exercises, and other games.** At large bookstores or specialty game stores, you can get some advice on which games are best. Also, playing bridge and other strategic card games can hone your critical thinking. Rumor has it that Bill Gates played lots of bridge in his short time at college.

Learning Target 6: Personal Accountability

Generations X and Y shy away from the downside of personalities with strong accountability issues. Yes, there is a downside if anything, even accountability, is taken too far. We have all known the coworker, almost always a Boomer, whose sense of responsibility has crossed the line and become a pain to all around him. He may be one of the following types of self-righteous, accountability enforcers:

He is self-righteous about all he does and knows he does too much, but his superior brand of accountability just forces him to go the limit and then some.

His standards of accountability must always be just a little bit higher than yours so that no one ever measures up. This does not make the employee a good team player, as he is not strong at appreciating the contributions of others.

He is the likeliest candidate for burnout and does not recognize when his productivity begins to falter as a result.

He grabs the lion's share of the work on projects and then complains or passive-aggressively shows resentment. He would rather take on too much responsibility than risk trusting others to do the thorough job he would do. This robs the team of developmental opportunities and a chance to make the group more productive.

He is always measuring and looking at what his peers or even you are doing and assessing where it falls short of his vision of what should be done. He wants credit to be assigned and touted when he has accomplished something. He wants people to know that he did tasks 1–6 while the rest of the team combined only did tasks 7–10. Not a good team dynamic.

As you can see, there are strong reasons many Generation X and Y managers don't want to be *that* guy. Even a more compelling reason is that most of the Gen-XY parents were strong on personal accountability in the workplace and made it look very unattractive to the younger generations. Often, the Boomer parents put work ahead of friends, family, and healthy lifestyle, so what they called personal accountability looked like a values deficit to Generations X and Y. Even though Boomer parents often felt they were working to benefit the family in terms of providing money for education, better housing, and a secure future, this did not feel like good family values to the latchkey kids the Boomer generation created.

And there are other reasons Generation X and Y managers are not as strong as Boomers on accountability:

Seeing the personal accountability Nazis alienate teammates makes younger managers walk wide circles around anything that looks like me, my, and I—even if it involves accountability.

The younger managers have career flexibility and are ready to be in the wind if a good opportunity pops up. This means that long-term commitments to stay and see a project through are just not going to happen.

From kindergarten on, a team approach has been taught by every school Gen-XYers attended. On the other hand, Boomers were taught "do your own work," "don't ask for outside help," "divide and conquer," "do more with less," and "more perspiration and less conversation." Boomers have been taught that when the going gets tough, the tough get going. Gen-XYers have been taught that when the going gets tough, rely on the resources of the team. For many that means that someone else will take up the slack. The concept of "it takes a village" to develop a child is applied to the workplace as well. It is easy to think that someone else will do it if your time is taxed and you feel you can't finish something. The problem is that everyone is busy today and some tasks are not getting done or getting done well or on time.

Gen-XYers are not so driven to see a finished product or project because throughout their careers they have seen projects axed midstream, approaches abandoned with frequent changes in leadership, and commitments broken because of events that are out of control. Ask anyone in the hospitality, nonprofit, or airline industry about changes post 9/11. Ask any younger employee whose parent left a good-paying job with a legacy company to participate in the dot-com bubble. Gen-XYers have strong reasons to believe that they should not be totally invested in seeing anything to a conclusion, because things can change dramatically overnight.

How to Achieve This Target

1. **Do your own inventory of your personal accountability.** Have any incidents or experiences in the past strongly demonstrated your sense of accountability? Do you or anyone else wish your sense of accountability had been stronger in a past

incident or situation? What could you have done to demonstrate greater accountability? If there are several incidents, try to determine if there is a common theme. Do you sometimes avoid accountability when you are overloaded? When you are asked to work with certain personality styles or departments? When you are new in a job?

2. **Ask for anonymous, candid feedback from your boss, your employees, your peers, and the people you serve.** Tell them you are working on personal accountability. Ask them if there is a task you could do better or more fully. It is important to get this 360-degree feedback, because sometimes a boss will think you are strong in executing tasks but your employees have a different experience, or vice versa. You may want to make out a form for them to fill out that looks something like this:

   A. On a scale of 1–5, 1 being highest and 5 being lowest, rate me on my strength in following through after committing to do something. ____

   B. Specifically, on a scale of 1–5, rate me on my strength in following through at the end of a project to finish well and tie up loose ends. ____

   C. On a scale of 1–5, how do I rate on taking initiative to take on responsibility? ____

   D. Please tell me below how I can improve in the area of personal accountability. If you have any examples, please include them, though this is not necessary.
   ____

3. **Look to outside groups to build a sense of personal accountability.** Service organizations like Kiwanis, churches and temples, and even Alcoholics Anonymous are all examples of groups that may have programs related to personal accountability, depending on the local leadership. Find out from current members if they think one of these groups would help you strengthen your personal accountability.

Retain the Best of the Boomer Generation

You wouldn't throw away all the valuable files and information on your current computer if you traded it in for a later model. Instead, you would review what was on the hard drive and back up files. Retaining the best from the minds, experiences, and work styles of the Boomer generation is even more important to your future success, both personally and organizationally.

Spend some time with the older workers who come your way in order to assess what they have to offer to fill any gaps in your own experience. Consider this a process of mentally backing up your existing knowledge base and expanding it to include the rich experience of your older colleagues. Blending the best of their generation and yours could aid in making you a truly great leader for employees of all ages.

APPENDIX

Bibliography

"The 2006 Cone Millennial Cause Study: The Millennial Generation: Pro-Social and Empowered to Change the World," Cone Inc., in collaboration with AMP Insights, 2006, *www.solsustainability.org*.

"AP-AOL Instant-Messaging Trends Survey," MarketingVOX: The Voice of Online Marketing, 16 November 2007, *www.marketingvox.com/archives/2007/11/16/ap-aol-instant-messaging-trends-survey-mobile-im-use-up*.

Armour, Stephanie, "Generation Y: They've Arrived at Work with a New Attitude," USA Today.com, 8 November 2005.

Bishop, John, "Are Your Managers Ready for Generation Y?" from Teaching Moments: Goal Setting for Students, 2007, *www.teachingmoments.com/want-proof.html*.

Burmeister, Misti, *From Boomers to Bloggers: Success Strategies Across Generations* (Fairfax, VA: Synergy Press, 2008).

Campbell, Kim, "The Many Faces of the Baby Boomers," *Christian Science Monitor*, 26 January 2005.

Christensen, Clayton M., "IM Usage in the US," UsageWatch.org, 21 September 2004, *www.usagewatch.org/2004/09/im_usage_in_the.html*.

Colon, Edna, "The Relation Between Generational Differences and Conflict Management Styles in a Telemarketing Call Center" (PhD diss., University of Phoenix, 2005).

Covey, Stephen R., *The 7 Habits of Highly Effective People* (New York, NY: Simon and Schuster, 1989).

DePree, Max, *Leadership Jazz* (New York, NY: Dell, 1993).

Eldrege, John, *Wild at Heart* (Nashville, TN: Nelson, 2001).

Erickson, Tammy, "Do You Want a Date or a Quart of Milk? More on Texting," Harvard Business Online, 3 July 2007, *http://discussionleader.hbsp.com/erickson/2007/07/do_you_want_a_date_or_a_quart_1.html.*

Erickson, Tammy, "'What Is It with You People and 8:30 A.M.?'"—Generation Y's First Impressions of Us," Harvard Business Online, 16 July 2007, *http://discussionleader.hbsp.com/erickson/2007/07/what_is_it_with_you_people_and_1.html.*

Families and Work Institute, "Generation and Gender in the Workplace" (published by American Business Collaboration, 2004), *http://familiesandwork.org/site/research/reports/genandgender.pdf.*

Gainsford, Len, "Generation Gap: Who's Afraid of Compliance?"*HR Magazine*, 13 June 2006, *www.humanresourcesmagazine.com.au/browse_news.asp?CatID=1223.*

Garrett, R. K., and J. K. Danziger, "IM = Interruption Management? Instant Messaging and Disruption in the Workplace," *Journal of Computer-Mediated Communication*, 20 October 2007.

Germaine, Jack, "IM at Work, Part 1: Idle Chatter, Serious Risk," *E-Commerce Times*, February–July 2004, *www.ecommercetimes.com.*

Gerber, Greg, "Generational Conflict," (Cygnus Interactive, 2006), quoting Karen and Troy Stendes, Stende Inspirations Inc.

Giancola, Frank, "The Generation Gap: More Myth Than Reality" Workforce and Human Resource Research, *Human Resource Planning Society*, 1 December 2006, *www.access-mylibrary.com/coms2/summary_0286-29180814_ITM.*

Greenberg, Anna, "How Generation Y Is Redefining Faith in the iPod Era," Reboot, 11 April 2005.

Kruger, Jennifer Barr, "Bridging the Generational Divide: Understanding Generational Differences in Your Workplace Can Lead to Higher Employee Morale and Greater Efficiency," *Photo Marketing*, 1 October 2002.

Massey, Morris, "Baby Boomer Versus Generation X: Managing the New Workforce," *Scribd*, *www.scribd.com/doc/38337/ TIPS-TO-IMPROVE-INTERACTION-AMONG-THE-GENERATIONS.*

Massey, Morris, *What You Are Is Where You Were When* (Cambridge, MA: Enterprise Media, 1986).

Pastore, Michael, "Instant Messaging Has Gone to Work," *The ClickZ Network*, 14 November 2001.

Perman, Stacy, "Best Entrepreneurs Under 25," *Business-Week*, 31 October 2005.

Petrovic, Vanja, "Will Grassroots Nonprofits Survive When Boomers Retire?" *AlterNet*, 7 August 2007, *www.alternet .org/workplace/5810.*

Putnam, Robert, *Bowling Alone: The Collapse and Revival of the American Community* (New York, NY: Simon and Schuster, 2000).

Robertson, Robin, "Leading Answers," 14 December 2006, *http://leadinganswers.typepad.com/leading_ answers/2006/12/verifying_motiv.html.*

Sebor, Jessica, "Y Me: Members of Generation Y Were the First to Mature in a Media-saturated, Tech-savvy World— Here's How to Blow Past the Buzz and Get the Brand into Their Brains," *CRM Magazine*.

"SHRM Generational Differences Survey Report: A Study by the Society for Human Resource Management," SHRM Surveys series, Society for Human Resource Management, 2005.

Smith, Gregory P, "Leaders Energize and Engage the Workforce," Chart Your Course International, 1 July 2008, *www.chartcourse.com/articleenergize.html.*

Thill, John V., and Courtland L. Bovee, *Excellence in Business Communication, 7th ed.* (New York, NY: Prentice Hall, 2006).

Wallace, Julie, "After X Comes Y—Echo Boom Generation Enters Workforce," *HR Magazine*, 1 April 2001.

Webster, Lee Ann H., "Sharpen Your Communication Skills," *BNET.com*, 1 September 2005.

Zust, Christine, MA, "Baby Boomer Leaders Face Challenges Communicating Across Generations," *www.emergingleader.com/article16.shtml.*

Index

About the Author

Casey Hawley conducts seminars on a wide range of communication and management topics to aid professionals of all ages to advance their careers. She is a frequent speaker for leadership development groups, especially those developing the talent of Generations X and Y to assume the executive positions of the future.

Casey is the author of five books, including *Effective Letters for Every Occasion, 100+ Strategies for Office Politics, 100+ Winning Answers to the Toughest Interview Questions,* and *200 Ways to Turn Any Employee into a Star Performer.*

Her Atlanta-based company, Casey Hawley Consulting, offers courses rated highly for both entertainment and long-term results. Some of the most popular topics include Career Change Management, Powerful Business Writing, Professional Development for Today, and Power Presentations.

Casey is a visiting instructor in the Marketing Department at Georgia State University and teaches in the Business Communication Department. The large urban university offers a diverse student population, many of whom are Generation X and Generation Y managers and professionals. Casey designed the interviews and survey for this book and they were conducted nationwide. Her daily consulting with younger managers and supervisors has also educated her regarding the unique challenges and visions of these leaders. Many of the solutions and innovations in this text are credited to Casey's younger clients and students.

Casey Hawley, MA, is a graduate of the University of Georgia. As a National Endowment for the Humanities Fellow, she conducted postgraduate work at Stanford University in the Department of Literature and Modern Thought. Her client list includes the Southern Company, Cox Communications, Equifax, Georgia-Pacific, and various governmental clients and churches. Her passions are prayer, teaching, creative writing, great business strategy, and her son.